Crimes Against Bureaucracy

Crimes Against Bureaucracy

ERWIN O. SMIGEL
New York University

H. LAURENCE ROSS
University of Denver

VAN NOSTRAND REINHOLD COMPANY
New York   Cincinnati   Toronto   London   Melbourne

Van Nostrand Reinhold Company Regional Offices:
Cincinnati   New York   Chicago   Millbrae   Dallas

Van Nostrand Reinhold Company Foreign Offices:
London   Toronto   Melbourne

Library of Congress Catalog Card Number 73-03979

Manufactured in the United States of America

Published by Van Nostrand Reinhold Company
450 West 33rd Street, New York, N. Y. 10001

Published simultaneously in Canada by
D. Van Nostrand Company (Canada), Ltd.

10   9   8   7   6   5   4   3   2   1

PREFACE

This book is concerned primarily with the nature of crime. It is addressed to students and professionals in criminology, the sociology of organizations, and the sociology of law. It is our hope that it will fulfill, at least partially, both teacher and student needs.

The book amplifies previous writers' perceptions that crime is a complex and varied phenomenon. Its characteristics change with the type of perpetrator, the type of victim, and the way in which the crime is carried out. Thus, theories of the cause and control of crime must be correspondingly complex and differentiated or they will be unrealistic and invalid. We hope that the insights provided in this volume on crimes committed against bureaucracies will be of use in the collective task of building a theoretical understanding of crime and criminals. It is unfortunate that so little work has been done in this particular area of criminology because no discussion of the field can be considered complete without its inclusion.

This collection also deals with the nature of bureaucracies. The pioneer work of Max Weber was instrumental in placing the study of bureaucracy within the scope of sociology. Research into the way that the individual confronts bureaucracy and the way that bureaucracy, in turn, confronts the individual is of particular interest today because of the increased concern of both laymen and professionals about the problematic relationship between individuals and organizations. This relationship has been characterized as one of alienation and depersonalization. The materials presented show that the relationship is also, routinely, one of criminal exploitation on the part of the individual against the bureaucracy.

v

We also consider the nature of law. Although the behavior reported here is formally subject to the traditional processes of criminal law, research has shown that crimes against bureaucracy are frequently treated by informal procedures, and the results are different from those which would be predicted from a knowledge of formal law alone. The studies included in this volume give cumulative evidence that the dry body of the law is often filtered through a gauze of ignorance, personal opinion, or practicality; thus significantly warping law enforcement procedures. The relationships we are dealing with have a basis in formal law, but are administered and substantively affected by informal and frequently unrecognized machinery. Here, as elsewhere, the law in action differs from the formal law in patterned and comprehensible ways. It is the duty of the sociologist to understand and describe these ways.

Finally, this compilation is concerned with the nature of social rules. The studies illustrate the paradox that criminal behavior relies on institutionalized rules in much the same way as conventional behavior does. In order to violate the commandment, "Thou shalt not steal," the violator must have recourse to other commandments which deflect the original rule or provide exceptions. Even the most serious, premeditated crime seems to require some social legitimation before it can be carried out.

CONTENTS

Crimes Against Bureaucracy

INTRODUCTION *

ERWIN O. SMIGEL

H. LAURENCE ROSS

The traditional discussion of crime among lawyers and criminologists, as well as among laymen, has been characterized largely by a stereotype: crime is assumed to be a matter of gross violation of ordinary social expectations, a deed of violence exemplified by murder, rape, and armed robbery. The criminal identified by this stereotype is typical of the inmates of a maximum-security prison: proletarian, disreputable, and pathological. Contemporary legislatures continue to prescribe traditional penalties regardless of the character of the violators. Contemporary psychology and sociology continue to search for pathological disturbances of the mind or of the social fabric that produce deviant personalities.

These practices based on stereotyped attitudes, though still current, are no longer credible and are increasingly being abandoned. The first major attack upon them came three decades ago

* We wish to thank Richard Quinney for his invaluable help in preparing this book. We are indebted to Joseph Bram, Albert K. Cohen, and Austin Turk for their comments on the draft manuscript and to Lucile D. Milberg and Janet W. Solinger for their editorial suggestions.

in the delineation of "white-collar crime" by Edwin H. Sutherland.[1] Sutherland was concerned with the extent to which businessmen generally, and corporations in particular, violated governmental rules and regulations in the course of their ordinary
business procedures. He demonstrated not only that corporations
and their executives commit criminal acts, but that this kind of
criminality is far more costly than is conventional crime.

From the viewpoint of theoretical criminology, the major
consequence of Sutherland's work was to cast doubt on simplistic
theories of crime causation. Criminological theories based on
poverty and ghetto neighborhoods or on psychological abnormali-
ties cannot explain criminal acts committed by business leaders.
Perhaps even more important in Sutherland's view, the task of
understanding the criminal is seen as that of understanding a
segment of behavior rather than a total personality. The criminal
is not an alien creature, governed in his behavior by strange or
special forces. Rather, he is the ordinary or even the respected
man, perhaps a pillar of the business community, who is doing
the job he thinks is expected of him.

While Sutherland and his followers attacked one oversimpli-
fication concerning the nature of crime, another group of contemporary criminologists demolished a second stereotype: that of
an active criminal and his innocent, passive victim. Perhaps the
landmark in this approach is *The Criminal and His Victim*, by
Hans von Hentig.[2] Von Hentig begins with the general sociological principle that a social relationship is a reciprocal phenomenon, involving the interrelated acts of at least two parties. A
crime can be viewed as a social relationship, involving both
criminal and victim. The victim has a definite role to play.[3] He
is not selected from a large population of law-abiding citizens by
mere chance. To be a victim, one must nearly always possess
some positive traits that distinguish him from the population of

[1] Edwin H. Sutherland, "White-Collar Criminality," *American Sociological
Review*, 5 (February, 1940), pp. 1–12; *White-Collar Crime*, New York:
Holt, Rinehart and Winston, 1949.

[2] Hans von Hentig, *The Criminal and His Victim*, New Haven: Yale University Press, 1948. See also: Steven Schafer, *The Victim and His Criminal:
A Study of Functional Responsibility*, New York: Random House, 1968.

[3] Marvin E. Wolfgang, "Victim-Precipitated Criminal Homicide," pp. 33–34;
Menachem Amis, "Patterns of Forcible Rape," pp. 60–75, in Marshall B.
Clinard and Richard Quinney, *Criminal Behavior Systems: A Typology*,
New York: Holt, Rinehart and Winston, 1967.

nonvictims. The average newspaper reader may surmise that a stroller in the park was robbed and beaten without reason; but the more astute observer notes that midnight strollers have a far higher chance of being mugged than noontime strollers, that pedestrians on a busy, well-lit street have a far lower chance of attack than those who choose deserted side streets for their perambulations.

Frequently, the victim participates even more directly. The con-man, for example, admits his inability to prey upon a truly honest man who would pass up the chance to get something for nothing. In crimes of prostitution and black-market transactions, the distinction between criminal and victim loses all usefulness. There is no meaningful way to distinguish between them, other than by the patterned inclination of law enforcement officers to arrest one party and ignore the other.

In this book we hope to continue to explore the avenues opened by Sutherland, Von Hentig, and their followers. We believe that one crucial element in the study of crime today lies not only in the respectability of the perpetrators, as Sutherland would have it, but also in the behavior of the victim, as Von Hentig suggests. In brief, we propose that, in addition to the nature of the criminal, the nature of the victim accounts for many of the features of an important type of crime in modern society. This type of crime we characterize as *crime against bureaucracy*. Although this phenomenon is brought to our attention regularly in the popular press, scholarly research has been limited. Our hope is that this treatise will stimulate further research which, in turn, will unearth new ways of looking at the criminal process.

BUREAUCRACY AS VICTIM

The victims with which we are concerned are organizations— corporate or governmental—which are large, impersonal, and dominated by formal rules and regulations. Following Max Weber,[4] we call these organizations *bureaucracies*. They are the

---

[4] The major characteristics of bureaucracy as described by Weber are listed in Peter Blau, *Bureaucracy in Modern Society,* New York: Random House, 1956, pp. 28–36. Briefly they are: a division of labor, a defined system of hierarchy of authority, a consistent system of abstract rules, impersonal detachment of the official in interpersonal relationships, hiring and promotion based on technical qualifications.

concentration points in our society of great wealth and power and, as such, are the popular victims of many contemporary property crimes. Although, as Sutherland showed, these organizations may be criminal in their own right,[5] we wish to make the point that they may also be victims. As victims, bureaucracies offer ambiguities to traditional conceptions of crime. The victim, usually an individual, is not, in the case of the bureaucracy.

However, bureaucratic procedures do involve people: officers, employees, suppliers, customers, and clients. The interest of many of these individuals in the welfare of the organization is minimal. In their relations with the bureaucracy a good portion of them encounter various inducements and opportunities to steal, to violate positions of trust, to commit some criminal act against the bureaucracy. We propose that the reasons they do so can be found in public attitudes toward bureaucracies and in the opportunity afforded by bureaucratic procedures.

The unpopularity of bureaucracies is a paradoxical fact in a society that depends on them for the provision of almost all goods and services. Among the reasons for this unpopularity are: the bureaucracy's impersonality in a society which still places a high value on personal relations; the conflict of interest between bureaucrats and the people they are expected to serve; and inefficiency in operation because of exaggerated emphasis on means (rules) instead of ends (goals) by workers in the bureaucracy.

In addition to being unpopular, bureaucracies are peculiarly vulnerable to types of criminal activity marked by low visibility. Thefts from bureaucracies often differ from conventional thefts in their subtlety. Unlike armed robbery, the theft of bureaucratic assets may involve an unobtrusive action, such as a shifting of numbers on a balance sheet, or falsification of reports and inventories. The crime of tax evasion, for example, can be accomplished within the confines of one's own home, without direct interaction with a member of the bureaucratic organization. Even the theft of physical goods, exemplified by shoplifting from a department store, can be carried out with a degree of unobtrusiveness that is very different from the types of crime envisaged by traditional criminology.

The low visibility of crimes against bureaucracies, combined with the unpopularity of the victims, leads to a failure of the

[5] *Cf.* Sutherland, *op. cit.*

public to stigmatize the perpetrators of these crimes. Even grand larceny may be quasi-legitimized as "chiseling," when the victim is a bureaucratic organization. The organization is denied access to an important source of protection afforded the personal victim: the sympathy and conscience of the general population.

This failure of the public to stigmatize crimes against bureaucracies leads, in turn, to another dilemma for the victims. Having apprehended a criminal, bureaucracies cannot routinely pass him on to official law enforcement agencies because the bureaucratic interest does not always coincide with a system of law enforcement based on the concept of a personal victim. The organization must retain a positive public image in order to avoid becoming an even more justifiable victim. Its interest, moreover, is in reimbursement more than retribution. Formal legal prosecution is also costly to the victim, in time and money. Consequently, bureaucratic organizations tend to develop their own systems of private dispositions, with remand to formal law enforcement being a sanction *in extremis.*

The extent of crime against bureaucracy has not been precisely measured, but indications are that it is widespread. A recent report of the President's Commission on Law Enforcement and the Administration of Justice[6] suggests that *income tax fraud,* in the form of failure to report income to the Federal Government, may be quite common. Estimates of unreported income range as high as $40 billion per year, some of which is deliberate crime. Local and state tax evasion would add considerably to these estimates. Data maintained by the American Bankers' Association indicate that banks lost about $15.3 million by *embezzlement* in 1965. The President's Commission estimates total embezzlement losses for all organizations at about $200 million per year.

Larceny from retail business, in the form of employee theft and shoplifting, is estimated at $1.3 billion annually. This figure does not include larceny from wholesale and industrial establishments. The American Bankers' Association estimates *forgery* losses on banking instruments at $60 million per year. The

[6] President's Commission on Law Enforcement and the Administration of Justice, *Crime and Its Impact—An Assessment,* Washington, D.C.: U.S. Government Printing Office, 1967, pp. 42–59.

Treasury Department estimated losses due to *counterfeiting* at $800 million in 1965.

There is a great deal of *robbery* directed against bureaucratic organizations. The President's Commission estimates that robbery of banks, retail and other commercial enterprises amounted to about $15.9 million in 1965. There was an estimated loss of $132.7 million in *burglary* from nonresidential premises.

With the exception of tax fraud and some cases of forgery and counterfeiting, the above figures do not include many offenses against government, such as "chiseling" from welfare agencies. Furthermore, the figures are based on official statistics and, as such, may underestimate the phenomenon. Many offenses against bureaucracies are probably undetected and never appear in official statistics. Moreover, the types of crime enumerated above do not include the traditional "white-collar crimes" committed against bureaucracies by other bureaucracies. Sutherland, Clinard, and others have documented the extensive losses resulting from these types of criminal acts.[7]

Crimes against bureaucratic victims constitute evidence for the view that criminality must be explained as a segment of the behavior of almost all men, rather than as an abnormality which distinguishes the criminal from the law-abiding citizen. If all men do not engage in crimes against bureaucracies, the vast majority see little or nothing wrong in certain kinds of crime against these victims. Moreover, the concentration of the society's wealth in bureaucratic hands continues, and this is likely to be accompanied by a continuing growth of property crimes against bureaucratic victims. Our understanding of crime and of the criminal must be enlarged to include this important and growing segment of law violation.

[7] Sutherland, *op. cit.*; Marshall B. Clinard, *The Black Market*, New York: Holt, Rinehart and Winston, 1952; Robert A. Lane, "Why Businessmen Violate the Law," *Journal of Criminal Law, Criminology and Police Science*, 44 (August, 1953), pp. 151–165; Gilbert Geis, "White Collar Crime: The Heavy Electrical Equipment Antitrust Cases of 1961," in Clinard and Quinney, *op. cit.*, pp. 139–151; John Herling, *The Great Price Conspiracy: The Story of the Antitrust Violations in the Electrical Industry*, Washington, D.C.: Robert B. Luce, 1962.

BUREAUCRACY AND PUBLIC OPINION

The size, wealth, and impersonality of big business and governments are attributes which make it seem excusable, according to many people, to steal from these victims. Theft appears to be easier to excuse when the victim has larger assets than the criminal, as exemplified by the Robin Hood myth. Congruent with this thesis is the tactic frequently used by bureaucracies: the attempt to "personalize" the loss. Witness this sign in a Midwestern motel: "If any towels are missing when you leave, the maid cleaning the room will be responsible for them." The notice attempts to deter theft by invoking sympathy for an individual rather than for the bureaucracy.[8] Some bureaucratic organizations, attempt to personalize the impersonal and to make the large corporation appear to be a family business.

Another reason why crimes against large organizations are more acceptable to the public than are other categories of crime may be that our system of ethics lacks rules which specifically apply to relationships between individuals and large organizations. All major historical religions originated in small communities, in which obligations concerned relatives, friends, and neighbors. From these static and personal communities a set of personal ethical norms developed; responsibility to great impersonal structures did not exist. Today, when large-scale organizations dominate our lives, men may be ethically unprepared to cope with the problem of the relationship between the individual and the corporation.

In addition to this lack of ethical tradition, there exists in Western culture an historic antipathy to the corporate idea. Abraham Chayes writes about the modern corporation: ". . . as it emerged from the seventeenth century it was by history and tradition at odds with the advancing spirit of individualism and

---

[8] Harry Gersh recounts an incident in which a group of Jewish ghetto children had stolen from a five-and-ten-cent store and brought the booty home, expecting to be praised for their success against what was called "the interests." To their surprise, they were soundly rebuked. It was pointed out that the girl behind the counter would be blamed. The elders explained that it was all right to "take" if the big, impersonal, wealthy "interests" bore the loss, but it was irrevocably wrong if an individual were made to suffer. "The Code According to Mama-Tante-Mom," *Commentary*, 13 (March, 1952), pp. 264–270.

rationalism." [9] This is still true, if Sloan Wilson, C. Wright Mills, and William H. Whyte are to be believed.[10]

There are other factors involved in the dislike of the large organization. A survey at the University of Michigan summarizes its findings concerning the public image of big business by noting that "the bulk of the arguments in disfavor can be reduced to criticism or distaste for big business's power or misuse of power over the worker, the competitor, the consumer, or other societal institutions." [11] Also, the large majority of people surveyed regarded big business profits as excessive.

Size and its concomitants of impersonality, bureaucratic power, and red tape are the main reasons given for the preference to steal from large organizations.[12] However, the relationship between size and stealing preference is not a simple one, for our culture is ambivalent toward bigness, rather than unalterably opposed. We boast about the size of our country, while we worry about the power of the central government; we are proud of our great corporations, yet we pass antitrust legislation to curb them. The Michigan survey found that people saw good as well as bad in big business, and, in fact, 76 per cent felt that the good outweighed the bad. Nevertheless, there is enough dislike for bigness and impersonality today to justify, for many, crime against large organizations.

OPPORTUNITY FOR CRIME AGAINST BUREAUCRACY

Bureaucracies are omnipresent in contemporary societies. Most people spend a great part of their daily lives in bureaucratic contexts. The opportunity to commit crimes against bureaucratic victims exists not only because of the ubiquity of bureaucracies,

[9] Abraham Chayes, "Introduction," in John P. Davis, *Corporations,* New York: Capricorn Books, 1961, p. 14.
[10] Sloan Wilson, *The Man in the Gray Flannel Suit,* New York: Simon and Schuster, 1955; C. Wright Mills, *The Power Elite,* New York: Oxford University Press, 1956; William H. Whyte, Jr., *The Organization Man,* New York: Simon and Schuster, 1956.
[11] Burton R. Fisher and Stephen B. Withey, *Big Business as the People See It: A Study of a Socioeconomic Institution,* Ann Arbor, Michigan: Institute for Social Research, University of Michigan, 1951.
[12] Erwin O. Smigel, "Public Attitudes Toward Stealing as Related to the Size of the Victim Organization," *American Sociological Review,* XXI, 3 (June, 1956), pp. 320–327 (reprinted in the present volume).

but also because of the ease with which criminal acts may be
accomplished, the low visibility of many offenses, the rationalizations available to the offenders, and the nature of bureaucratic
response to victimization. Individuals may have various relationships to bureaucratic
organizations: employee, consumer, supplier, taxpayer, and oth-
ers. These relationships present various inducements and opportunities for criminal actions. Employees, for example, may be
motivated to steal from their bureaucratic employers because
they feel that their work is insufficiently rewarded or unfairly
demanding, or that the organization fails to live up to ideal standards. Close contact with company property under varying degrees
of security offers them opportunity to steal. Evasion of bureaucratic regulations depends directly on the amount and degree of
supervision and the felt repressiveness of the rules. Income tax
violation, check forgery, and shoplifting occur in bureaucratic
relationships other than employment or supervision, each illus-
trating a different set of opportunities for crime provided by various relationships.[13]

THE "CRIMINAL" [14]

Most individuals who steal from bureaucracies differ from more
stereotyped criminals in that they lack criminal records and criminal self-conceptions. In an examination of the most flagrant cases
of wartime price-control and rationing violations, it was found
that fewer than one in ten of the violators had any kind of criminal record.[15] Shoplifters in a large Chicago department store,
when arrested, would not admit that their behavior constituted

[13] Harold M. Groves, "Empirical Studies of Income Tax Compliance," *National Tax Journal*, 11 (December, 1958), pp. 291–301 (reprinted in part
in the present volume); Edwin M. Lemert, "An Isolation and Closure
Theory of Naive Check Forgery," *Journal of Criminal Law, Criminology
and Police Science*, 44 (September–October, 1953), pp. 296–307; Mary
Owen Cameron, *The Booster and the Snitch: Department Store Shoplifting*,
New York: The Free Press of Glencoe, 1964 (reprinted in part in the present volume).
[14] For a more detailed discussion of the nature of one kind of crime against
bureaucracy, see Erwin O. Smigel, "Public Attitudes Toward 'Chiseling'
with Reference to Unemployment Compensation," *American Sociological
Review*, XVIII, 1 (February, 1953), pp. 59–67 (reprinted in the present
volume).
[15] Clinard, *op. cit.*

theft.[16] Cressey noted that among embezzlers, "the accountants, bankers, business executives and independent businessmen all reported that the possibility of stealing or robbing to obtain the needed funds never occurred to them, although many objective opportunities for such crimes were present."[17] The embezzlers were subsequently able to rationalize their acts on the basis that other people in business were doing similar things. In fact, Cressey found that such rationalizations were a necessary step in the process of embezzlement. It is likely that other persons who commit crimes against bureaucracies also define the situation as noncriminal. At least, they are able to regard their conduct as not inappropriate, given their conceptions of the nature of the victim.

BUREAUCRATIC VICTIMS AND THE CRIMINAL PROCESS

A strong argument has been made that certain crimes against bureaucracies are fundamentally different from traditional crime, in that they involve laws that are merely "economic regulations."[18] The crimes discussed in this book are not of this order. Our principal concern is with the thefts perpetrated mainly by individuals upon corporate, governmental, and other bureaucracies. The amounts stolen are enormous, especially so in comparison to the amounts stolen from personal victims.[19] These acts generally fall squarely within traditional criminal law, and they are subject to ordinary criminal procedure.

Despite the similarities between crimes against bureaucracies and those against other victims, the former are infrequently the subject of the formal criminal process. Few of the perpetrators are prosecuted, and of those convicted, few are punished with imprisonment.[20] The reasons for the differential treatment re-

[16] Cameron, *op. cit.*, pp. 161–163.
[17] Donald R. Cressey, *Other People's Money*, New York: The Free Press of Glencoe, 1953 (reprinted in part in the present volume), p. 140.
[18] Sanford H. Kadish, "Some Observations on the Use of Criminal Sanctions in Enforcing Economic Regulations," *University of Chicago Law Review*, 30 (Spring, 1963), pp. 423–449.
[19] Norman Jaspan and Hillel Black, *The Thief in the White Collar*, Philadelphia: J. B. Lippincott, 1960.
[20] President's Commission on Law Enforcement and the Administration of Justice, *op. cit.*, pp. 48, 113–114; Gerald D. Robin, "Corporate and Judicial Disposition of Employee Thieves," *Wisconsin Law Review*, 3 (Summer, 1967), pp. 685–702 (reprinted in the present volume).

ceived seem to be in large part related to the type of criminal involved and to the nature of the bureaucratic victim. Often the theft is unobtrusive, as when the thief occupies a position of responsibility. Embezzlement is one example. The collection of income tax from self-employed persons presents an analogous situation in which large numbers of individuals are responsible for their own compliance, and the violation of this trust is commonplace. The President's Commission on Law Enforcement and the Administration of Justice notes:

The crime [of tax fraud] is usually committed in the privacy of the home or office, without eyewitnesses or physical traces. While many white-collar crimes of misrepresentation have victims who may provide evidence—e.g. competitors, consumers, investors, stockholders—tax fraud has none. The inferences required to prove a tax fraud case must commonly be drawn from events largely independent of the commission of the crime and within control of the offender . . .[21]

Even the more blatant forms of crimes against bureaucracy may be difficult to discover because they may be completely or partly legitimized within a subgroup. The difficulty of detection of crimes against bureaucracies fosters the development of specialized private departments charged with the responsibility of discovering theft and dealing with the accused.[22] These departments can develop specialized procedures and sources of information not available to the unspecialized public police. The department store Protection Department and the Internal Revenue Service Intelligence Division replace the personal victim in the functions of experiencing criminal acts and bringing them to formal attention. Of course, even personnel charged with these responsibilities may themselves violate their trust, and thus create a particularly difficult problem of detection.

Hence, a major reason for the lack of formal handling of crimes against bureaucracies is that these crimes are difficult to discover. These crimes are seldom discovered by public authorities. Rather, they are discovered by officials of the bureaucracies, particularly the private police, who may choose to prosecute

[21] President's Commission on Law Enforcement and the Administration of Justice, *op. cit.*, p. 113.
[22] Cameron, *op. cit.*

formally or to handle the matter in an informal way. Of course, a similar choice exists in crimes against individuals; the victim may decide upon a private remedy rather than inform the police. However, personal victims seem to be motivated by their adherence to the legal system generally and by the personal satisfaction gained through the legal punishment of the offender. Personal victims, moreover, seldom have a major stake in any private disposition they might be able to make with the offender. The bureaucracy, in contrast, may be able to obtain recompense and prevent further loss by informal procedures, such as requiring the return of stolen property and the resignation or discharge of offending personnel. These gains may be forfeited by recourse to prosecution, which involves the loss of working time by the testifying staff; and, thus in a way, continues the victimization of the bureaucracy. Bureaucracy does not feel indignant or outraged in the presence of theft. It does experience financial loss, but this loss may be passed on to another: for example, an insurance company or the consumer. Even when it does experience financial loss, if some restitution is made and the employee dismissed, the shoplifter permanently barred from the premises, or the tax evader placed under constant surveillance, the bureaucracy's interest in the incident fades.

Another reason for the lack of formal handling is the inefficiency of criminal procedure in many instances. As noted above, the crimes are often subtle and the evidence concerning their commission may involve complex technical information. The evidence necessary for criminal conviction may thus be difficult to obtain and to present to a jury, whereas much less justification is needed for informal handling. Many employees accused of dishonesty would be acquitted in court on the basis of insufficient evidence. The formally acquitted suspect in crimes like shoplifting could then bring a civil suit to harass the organization further. Even when formal criminal proceedings are instituted, the likelihood of imprisonment is slight, perhaps reflecting the fact that people who steal from bureaucracies seldom have the criminal records or display the violent behavior that seem to incline some judges toward prison sentences. Perhaps the lenient treatment also reflects the lenient public attitudes toward those criminals whose victims are bureaucracies.

THE SELECTIONS

The first two articles, by Erwin O. Smigel, deal with public attitudes toward stealing from bureaucracies. Small business, large business, government, and, as a separate illustration, the unemployment compensation system are the entities studied. The data show that it would be an exaggeration to say that stealing from bureaucracies is condoned by the public, but the degree of condemnation is much less than might be expected had the traditional categories of victim been studied. Furthermore, the larger and more bureaucratic the victims, the greater the willingness to approve stealing. Failure to disapprove strongly of stealing is a function of the bureaucratic nature of the victim, lack of knowledge (of illegality, in particular), exigency and other competing norms, and the low socioeconomic status of the respondent.

The next two selections, by Donald N. M. Horning and Donald R. Cressey, indicate some of the ways in which those who steal from bureaucracies manage to avoid self-definition as criminals. This avoidance facilitates the crime. As Cressey shows, the attitudes involved are not peculiar to the criminals, but are taken from the larger cultural context and involve general attitudes toward property and the bureaucratic setting. Horning finds that in a factory the workers identify three classes of property: personal, corporate, and property of uncertain ownership. Items which are small in size, plentiful, inexpensive, and not subject to an established accounting procedure tend to fall into this latter category. Pilfering these items is not considered to be theft, provided that the intended use is personal and not commercial. Cressey finds that a definition of the act as not ordinary theft, is essential for embezzlement to occur. The three successful rationales are: that the behavior is essentially noncriminal; that it is justified; or that it is part of a general irresponsibility for which the embezzler is not completely accountable. The inability of some embezzlers to see themselves as criminals extends even into the penitentiary, where they were interviewed.

The fifth selection, by Harold Groves, shows the relationship between stealing from bureaucracy and opportunity, in terms of visibility of the offense to agencies of control. Groves calculates the gross rents that in theory should be reported as income from rental property by interviewing the tenants of a sample of residential units. He compares this with the amounts actually reported to the state taxing authority. The ratio of reported to estimated rent declines with visibility of the rental relationship. Gross income from rental of multiple dwellings is fairly well reported, whereas that from renter sublets is very much underreported. Groves then estimates the likely maintenance costs of the buildings and deducts these from gross rentals to form an estimate of net return. This again is compared with the figures reported by the landlords to the taxing authority. Even in the best-reported category, the income declared is barely half of what it is calculated to be, and in the less visible cases the proportion of compliance is extremely low.

The sixth selection, by Mary Owen Cameron, discusses the manner in which one type of bureaucracy, a department store, deals with prevention, detection, and disposition of one type of criminal—the shoplifter. The operation of the private police is explained in a manner that illustrates the peculiar expertise that is developed in response to the specialized nature of the crime.

The final selection, by Gerald Robin, describes how a department store handles the problem of dishonest employees. Prosecution in this case, as with the shoplifters described by Cameron, is very rare. Robin finds that it is not the fear of reprisal that brings about this situation, but rather the desire to avoid the publicity that might mar the company image. The usual punishment, then, is discharge. When prosecution is undertaken, the record of conviction is very high. However, the punishments inflicted by the courts are very light: less than five per cent of those found guilty are given jail sentences, and the median fine is less than $50. Robin speculates that judges believe that there is little that the present system of handling criminals can do to reform or rehabilitate the offenders, and so the courts choose not to be punitive toward otherwise respectable people whose crime consists of stealing from bureaucratic employers.

PUBLIC ATTITUDES TOWARD STEALING AS RELATED TO THE SIZE OF THE VICTIM ORGANIZATION *

ERWIN O. SMIGEL

This study concerns attitudes toward stealing from each of three categories of organizations: small business, large business, and government. It was conducted in an effort to determine how size of the victim organization affects public attitudes toward stealing. The study seemed important not only for the immediate issue, but also for possible insights into attitudes toward bureaucracy, especially its impersonal aspects, and for what it could add to an understanding of the relationship between organizational size and attitudes in general. Usual assumptions pertaining to the effect of organizational size on attitudes suggest the following hypothesis: If obliged to choose, most individuals would prefer to steal from, and be more approving of others stealing from, large-scale, impersonal rather than from small-scale, personal organizations.[1]

* *American Sociological Review*, Vol. 21, No. 3, June, 1956. Revision of a paper read at the Third International Congress on Criminology, September, 1955. This research was supported by a grant from the Graduate School of Indiana University.

[1] That individuals sometimes see large-scale organizations as personal organizations is recognized. In the present study, however, this perception was

To explore this hypothesis a systematic random sample of 212 non-transient adults of Bloomington, Indiana, was drawn and interviewed in their homes. These individuals, in addition to background information queries, were given fifteen hypothetic situational questions,[2] a set of five for each type of organization, involving stealing from government, large business, and small business.[3] The respondents were asked to approve or disapprove, using Likert scale categories, of stealing under a variety of circumstances. The first section of this paper analyzes situational question responses.[4] A second section examines responses to a forced choice hypothetical circumstance query. Respondents were requested to select the one organization—government, large business, or small business—from which they would prefer to steal if forced by necessity. They were then asked to give reasons for their selection or rejection of each organization.

---

seldom verbalized, due in part to the fact that the respondents were not given specific organizations to consider and so had to call on their generalized experience, rather than a specific name stimulus, in order to visualize the types of organizations mentioned in the questionnaire.

[2] The situations were constructed so that respondents with a sixth-grade education, or the equivalent, could read and understand them. Readability level was determined by the Flesch test and the usual interview pretest. The entire questionnaire is available on request. A sample of the situational questions follows:

"Bill Terr, a World War II veteran, went to school on the GI Bill. While there, the government overpaid him $89 on his subsistence allowance. He did not report this error."

"Richard Smith's house burned. He is protected by fire insurance; however, when he filed his claim for insurance, he claimed damages greater than he actually had."

"John Charles went to his local cleaner to pick up a suit he had cleaned. The clerk was busy and asked John to find his own clothing. John found his suit and paid for it. He discovered later that he also had taken a pair of trousers that did not belong to him. He decided not to return them."

Many of the fifteen situational questions are usually regarded as crime from a legal standpoint but are often thought of as less serious than traditional crime and sometimes more lightly termed "chiseling."

[3] The questions concerning government, large business, and small business were rotated and mixed within each unit. No distinction arose because of the order of the questions.

[4] Three situational questions, one for each of the organizations under consideration, were judged to be equivalent. The other questions, designed to cover similar situations, make no claim for equivalence. The manner in which equivalence was determined is described in a previous article. See Erwin O. Smigel, "Public Attitudes Toward 'Chiseling' with Reference to Unemployment Compensation," *American Sociological Review*, 18 (February, 1953), p. 61 (reprinted in this volume).

THE SITUATIONAL QUESTION ANALYSIS

Cross correlations between each of the organizations indicate that respondents generally disapprove of stealing regardless of the size of the organization. Despite this general disapproval, important differences in degree of disapproval were found. The Stealing Attitude Scores (Table 1) show greatest disapproval

Table 1
Attitudes Toward Stealing

Stealing Attitude Scores	Type of Organization					
	Government		Large Business		Small Business	
	N	per cent	N	per cent	N	per cent
6–10 (Strongly approve to approve)	(0)	0	(2)	1	(0)	0
11–15 (approve to indifferent)	(13)	6	(7)	3	(5)	2
16–20 (indifferent to disapprove)	(133)	63	(129)	61	(101)	48
21–25 (disapprove to strongly disapprove)	(66)	31	(73)	34	(106)	50
Total	(212)	100	(212)[1]	100	(212)	100

1 Includes one case not tabulated.

toward stealing from small business and lesser disapproval toward stealing from large business and government. Although differences in degree of disapproval between large business and government are negligible, the results, at least for the large versus small dichotomy, support the hypothesis.

When the Stealing Attitude Scores of people with various backgrounds are compared, some further differentiation is discovered. In terms of socio-economic status it was found that regardless of organizational size, the lower the SES, the greater the approval of stealing.[5] Similar results were obtained by separate

[5] *Ibid.*, pp. 65–67. This finding is consistent with attitudes concerning "chiseling" unemployment compensation from the government. However, this lesser disapproval on the part of lower SES respondents probably does not justify any conclusions about a greater morality on the part of the upper classes.

analysis of occupation and education. In general, on Counts' occupational scale, respondents who rated lower were more approving than were those who rated higher. The same consistency was found in connection with level of education. Respondents with less than thirteen years of schooling were less disapproving of stealing than were those with more education.

Although relationships between approval or disapproval and social class exist, the various socio-economic levels seem to be affected differentially by the size of the victim organization. Table 2 demonstrates that lower socio-economic respondents

Table 2

Differences in Attitudes of Respondents from Two Socio-Economic Levels: Percentages Who Strongly Disapprove of Stealing

SES Level	N	*Victim Organization*			Proportional Difference[1]
		SB	LB	GOV	
		per cent	per cent	per cent	
Upper	(62)	58	42	42	38
Lower	(146)	46	31	26	77
Both SES Levels	(208)	50	34	31	61
Unclassified	(4)				
Total Sample	(212)				

1 Difference between GOV and SB over GOV per cents times 100.

show the greatest proportional difference in scores between government and small business.[6] A 77 per cent proportional difference resulted for lower SES as compared with 38 per cent for upper respondents, indicating the differential effect of organizational size upon subjects' attitudes. Respondents, then, from lower socio-economic levels, are more affected by size of organization than are those from upper levels.

Comparable relationships of the following sort were also found:

1. SEX Stealing Attitude Scores for the sample of 110 men and 102 women differ, with females more inclined to approve of steal-

[6] These figures were arrived at by taking the difference in scores between government and small business, and using the government score, which was usually the least disapproving, as the base.

ing than males. However, men who approved did so to a greater degree than did women. Analysis of the differences in scores between government and small business, for both men and women, in the most disapproving column (21–25) testifies that size of the victim organization also affects men differently than women. Females, although more approving of stealing, showed the greatest proportional attitudinal difference against stealing when small business is the victim: 67 per cent compared to a 54 per cent difference for men.

2. RELIGIOSITY Analysis of religiosity and Stealing Attitude Scores indicates nominally religious respondents as more critical of stealing than respondents not claiming religion. Examination of the most disapproving category reveals no change in the proportionate difference of attitude from government to small business. However, non-religious respondents were least disapproving of stealing from large business. Comparison between low disapproval and high disapproval scores for religious and non-religious respondents, using large business as the base for non-religious subjects in this instance, indicates that non-religious interviewees show the greatest proportional difference: 81 per cent as against 56 per cent for religious respondents.

3. VETERANS Although male veterans of World War II were more approving of stealing than were male non-veterans,[7] veterans were more affected by size of the victim organization. Comparison of differences between government scores and small business scores shows that veterans differed 86 per cent; non-veterans only 47 per cent.

Note has been taken that: (1) Nearly all respondents disapproved of the stealing behavior outlined in the situational questions, regardless of size of the victim organization. (2) Intensity of disapproval varied with size of the organization. Respondents were more disapproving of stealing from small business than from large business or government. (3) Further variations in attitudes were related to other social elements such as SES, sex, religiosity and group membership. (4) Additional differences in attitudes as affected by organizational size were observed within each of these social units. (5) The influence on stealing attitudes

---

[7] This finding did not hold for veterans of previous wars whose resocialization to a civilian way of life is probably more complete.

of any one background classification seems to depend on its relationship to one or more classifications.

FORCED CHOICE STEALING PREFERENCE

To arrive at the basis for these differences in attitudes, each respondent was asked to choose the type of organization from which he would rather steal if in need and he felt he had no other choice. Interviewees were then requested to explain their preference. In general respondents remained faithful to their strong disapproval of stealing from small business. However, the forced stealing question produced an altered order of stealing approval: large business now became the preferred first choice, then government and finally small business. The forced stealing choice reveals more than a change in order; of greater significance is the large number who preferred to steal from large business rather than from government as compared to the negligible difference in approval between large business and government when the situational questions were employed. Now 102 respondents preferred to steal from large business; 53 from government; and 10 from small business. Of the remaining subjects nine did not distinguish between large business and government, five did not differentiate at all, thirty refused to steal under any condition and three would not answer the question.

Respondents who made a stealing choice used two basic lines of reasoning to explain their preference—these involved consideration of the principles of least evil and/or least risk. The majority had registered their disapproval of stealing when they answered the situational questions. The selection question forced them to make a stealing preference for themselves. This placed them in a situation many found objectionable. To modify this position, most respondents decided from which organization stealing was the lesser evil before choosing their victim.

The second major line of reasoning involved the principle of least risk. The possibility of being caught and punished for theft seems to have a strong influence on stealing preference. However, this reasoning often runs counter to the first. Respondents who conceive of the problem in terms of both concepts and who cannot integrate them must weigh and evaluate the principle of lesser evil against the principle of least risk. Although these themes run through most of the reasons advanced by respondents for their stealing, different categories of interviewees see these ideas in different ways. An analysis of these various categories of stealing preference and reasons advanced for stealing choice in its relationship to size of the victim organization follows.

SMALL BUSINESS AS THE PREFERRED VICTIM

Of the 212 respondents, only eight men and two women preferred to steal from small business. Their mean scores for the situational questions are slightly lower than those of subjects in other categories, and they show a greater predisposition toward cheating small business than do other respondents. This is the only category where the mean score for small business is not the most disapproving score. The order of mean scores from the most disapproving to the least disapproving for these individuals is: large business 20.0, small business 19.5 and government 18.6 (the most disapproving score for each classification is 25).

Their reasons for choosing small business as the potential victim were relatively simple and direct. Selection was made mainly on the principle of the least risk. Even if caught, these respondents felt that the small businessman, who was on personal terms with his customers, would be more lenient than the managers of large business or government. A woman respondent put it: "The small businessman would be more human; he would give you a break. Big businessmen are cold-blooded and the government, of course, might catch you."

The risk factor seemed to operate as a deterrent for these respondents. They did not feel more justified in cheating small business as against the other organizations, but they perceived the situation as involving the least risk. Only one respondent felt morally justified in stealing from small business. Most were afraid of the consequences of stealing from large-scale organizations. Government especially inspired the fear of being caught and sentenced. The replies indicate that were it not for the fear of punishment, these individuals might have preferred to steal from the larger organizations. Their use of the principle of least risk seems to run counter to the original hypothesis which implies that the respondents would be more kindly disposed toward personal small business than toward impersonal large business.

However, the findings revealed that though the personal element is recognized, it is evaluated in conjunction with fear of discovery and punishment. For these respondents the principle of least risk seems to have more importance for their decisions on stealing than the principle of least evil.

LARGE BUSINESS AS THE PREFERRED VICTIM

One hundred and two members of the sample preferred to steal from large business. The overwhelming popularity of this type of organization reverses the disapproval order elicited by the situational questions. The mean scores for these questions indicated only minor attitudinal differences, especially between government and large business: 20.8 for small business, 19.6 for large business and 19.4 for government.

The forces making for favorable attitudes toward stealing from large-scale business seem more complex than those involved in creating similar attitudes toward small business. Many reasons for and against stealing from large business were offered. Some involved conflicts of values which were difficult to resolve. Most respondents based their choice of large business as the victim on the principle of lesser evil, feeling that stealing from big business was not as bad as stealing from small business because large business was impersonal, powerful and ruthless.[8]

While few respondents specifically mentioned the term "impersonal," they often implied it: "They're corporations." "Big business deals with you at arm's length; you can deal with it in the same way." For some, bigness and impersonality bred resentment and distrust. Two grounds were offered for this feeling; one concerned weakness generally associated with bureaucracy, the other the notion that big business is ruthless. Reasons advanced under the first classification claimed that large business wasted time, space, and energy. Second category reasons were more varied, for example: "I'm more callous toward big business because they're more ruthless." "After all they cheat you." "Why don't they pay a living wage?"

[8] For an interesting article which distinguishes between stealing from impersonal organizations and the individual, see: Harry Gersh, "The Code According to Mama-Tante-Mom," *Commentary*, 13 (March, 1952), pp. 264–270.

Many regarded big business profits as excessive and this be-lief was used by some as a basis for their resentment.[9] Examples are numerous: "They have the highest margin of profits and can afford the loss better; besides they allow for it." "Big business has

Table 3
Primary Reasons for Preferring to Steal from Large Business

Reasons for Stealing Choice	N	per cent
Can afford it best, or has tremendous capital	(69)	67.7
Allows for it: raises prices, is insured	(13)	12.8
They cheat you; they're ruthless	(8)	7.8
Less chance of being caught	(4)	3.9
Provides the greatest opportunity	(3)	2.9
No reasons offered	(5)	4.9
Total	(102)	100.0

tremendous capital, a part of which they've cheated from me." Distrust and resentment of big business led 21 per cent of the individuals who would rather steal from large business to apply the "eye for an eye" principle in making their decision. They believed that big business robbed them either by outright theft, or by charging exorbitant prices. In either event, this "be-havior" on the part of large business provided justification for those who chose to steal from large business since they con-sidered this decision the lesser evil. Another 68 per cent legiti-mated their preference for victimizing large business on a "Robin Hood" philosophy. For them robbing the rich to give to the poor —in this instance themselves—was a lesser evil.

Some preferences appeared based mainly on the principle of least risk. In all, seven per cent believed that large business pro-vided more opportunity for theft with less chance of discovery or punishment. The anonymity of big business is believed to offer greater opportunity for stealing from large business rather than small business. The choice between the two large-scale organiza-tions was made in favor of large business as the victim because of the respondents' greater fear of government. As one man

[9] For a larger picture of public attitudes toward big business, see: Burton R. Fisher and Stephen B. Withey, *Big Business as the People See It*, The Survey Research Center Institute for Social Research, University of Michi-gan: 1951.

expressed it: "There is no sense stealing from the government because the FBI is smarter than the police."

Grounds for stealing preference, even in the abstract, have
been presented as if they were mutually exclusive, as if there
were not a multiplicity of reasons which had to be considered
and weighed before decision could be made. This is not so. The
impersonality, the inconsiderate materialism, the opportunity offered by the anonymity big business provided were among the
elements in favor of choosing large business. Many individuals
who extended these reasons also had "cause" for not preferring
large business, such as admiration for the big businessman, or
intense dislike for government, or the belief that the small businessman might be more lenient if he caught them. Special diffi-

Table 4

**Reasons for Not Stealing from Government and Small Business, by
Respondents Who Chose Large Business as the Victim[1]**

Government		
Reasons for Not Stealing from Government	*N*	*per cent*
It's stealing from yourself	(23)	29.5
Would get caught by GOV and penalty might be stiffer	(18)	23.1
Needs its money	(15)	19.2
Stealing from GOV affects other citizens in the community	(13)	16.7
Patriotism	(7)	9.0
Lack of opportunity	(2)	2.5
Total	(78)	100.0

Small Business		
Reasons for Not Stealing from Small Business	*N*	*per cent*
SB does not have too much money	(42)	76.3
Identification: small like yourself, or member of community	(8)	14.6
Might know small businessman	(5)	9.1
Total	(55)	100.0

1   Figures in this table do not equal 102 for each division, GOV and SB, since all respondents
did not offer negative reasons for their stealing preference.

culty arose when decision had to be made between large business and government where both organizations were considered big and both stand accused of bad bureaucratic practices. Generally, however, grounds for preferring to steal from large business were related to reasons for not stealing from small business. One combination of reasons reads: "A man has to be very small to take from the little man. Large business can afford it. If you clip government, you just clip yourself, and what's more, you have a good chance of being caught." Table 4 shows the relative frequency of these reasons.

The data presented for this category again point out that while bigness and its corollaries play important parts in affecting the decision to steal from large business, these factors alone were often not sufficient to determine this choice. Many other reasons were offered. The pro and con of the particular choice appears to have been considered before final decision was made, and the principles of lesser evil and least risk run through the majority of the reasons proffered.

GOVERNMENT AS THE PREFERRED VICTIM

Fifty-three members of the 212 sample chose to steal from government. Their mean scores (20.9 for small business, 20.2 for large business, and 19.5 for government) for the situational questions are slightly higher than those for respondents who chose small business or large business. The mean scores demonstrate that members of this category both preferred to steal from government and were less disapproving of others stealing from government.

The task of choosing a victim appears less complicated for these individuals than for those who preferred to steal from large business, but more complicated than for those who elected to steal from small business. Fewer secondary reasons for their choice were offered. Clear-cut primary reasons often coincided with reasons for not stealing from either small business or large business. Intense dislike for government also helped make for definite preferences.

All of the reasons for stealing listed in Table 5 involve the theme of lesser evil. Most of the 32 per cent who thought that government could best afford the loss felt also that what they

Table 5
Respondents' Primary Reasons for Preferring to Steal From Government

Reasons	N	per cent
Can afford it best, or collects a great amount of tax money	(17)	32.1
Taking back own money	(8)	15.1
Government's function to take care of the needy	(7)	13.2
Against Democratic Administration[1]	(7)	13.2
Bureaucratic inefficiencies	(5)	9.4
Everybody does it	(5)	9.4
Distributes the loss	(4)	7.6
Total	(53)	100.0

1 The data for this study were collected in 1951 and 1952 while the Democratic administration was in power.

might take would not hurt it to the extent that similar thefts would affect smaller organizations. This notion is subscribed to by an additional eight per cent who believed that stealing from government was the lesser evil because the loss was well distributed. The choice was further justified on grounds that a great deal of money was collected in taxes; some of this taxation, it was hinted, was unnecessary. Many argued, then, that government was big and wealthy and stated their preference in terms of the "Robin Hood" principle.

Bureaucracy, which was equated to size and disfunctioning, was an additional justification for the choice of government as the victim. Although this type of criticism was leveled against large business, it was more frequently applied to government. Such items as waste and red tape were not uncommon grounds for stealing preference. Only 9 per cent of this category preferred this as their primary reason, but many others mentioned bureaucratic inefficiencies as a secondary reason. That bigness and its corollaries played a part in determining this choice is seen in the following examples: "Government is the bigger concern; it wouldn't hurt government as bad as an individual or smaller concern." "They waste anyhow; they throw away more than I would take."

Though government is generally conceived of as larger than large business, the section of Table 4 dealing with government indicates the importance of factors other than size as a determinant of choice for some respondents. Concepts of loyalty, patriotism and fear of government swayed many individuals to select large business rather than government. Yet, size was still important for many of those who chose to steal from government.

The bigness of government, however, does not account for all who elected it as the victim. Lesser evil may be premised on factors other than bigness, and the 13 per cent who were against the Democratic administration grounded their judgment on this theme. Their feelings are reflected in such statements as: "I'm anti-socialist." "It's a God damned government anyway—if it were O.K., I'd take from big business."

Another category felt that stealing from government was the lesser evil because the respondents were part of the government and had contributed to its support. They reasoned that stealing from government would be stealing from themselves, and so less criminal. These individuals were among the most difficult to force into a decision involving their possible stealing. Their scores on the situational questions were among the most disapproving. They selected government reluctantly and only because they felt this choice was the least dishonest.

An additional 13 per cent, whose scores on the situational questions were also very disapproving, thought that it was government's function to take care of the needy. These individuals intimated that if government failed in its duty, they were then more justified in stealing from it.

The following generalizations seem to be indicated: (1) While bigness and impersonality played a part in determining the preference for government as the victim, these elements do not seem as important for this category as they did for large business. (2) Other factors with strong emotional overtones— loyalty, patriotism, even anti-administration sentiment—appear to affect the decisions of some of the respondents. (3) Making decisions for this category seems easier than for those who chose large business, but not as easy for those who selected small business. (4) Enough reasons pro and con were advanced so that the weighing process noted in the selection of large business was evident once again. (5) Some of the same reasons for preferring to steal from large business were again in evidence for those who selected government.

While most respondents disapproved of stealing from any of

the organizations, differences in intensity of disapproval exist. Attitudes against stealing from small business were the most intense. Differences in attitudes, however, were also found on the basis of other social elements: socio-economic status, sex, religiosity, and group membership. These differences were in turn variously affected by size of the victim organization. In general, public attitudes toward a number of situational questions indicate that while size of organization does affect attitudes toward stealing, it is by no means the only factor.

When interviewees were "forced" to choose a victim organization, they weighted their selection in the following order: large business, government, and small business. The reasons offered for their decision generally involved the principles of least risk and lesser evil. Those who chose to steal from small business reasoned on the basis of least risk; those who preferred large business invoked both principles, but emphasized the lesser evil; while those who chose government overwhelmingly reasoned on the basis of the lesser evil.

Size and its concomitants, anonymity, impersonality, bureaucratic inefficiency, and power seem to play a major part in their decision. This supports the general hypothesis; yet other elements such as fear of capture and punishment, patriotism, and not wanting to cheat oneself also enter the picture. Further research in this area should prove fruitful. The relationship between size and stealing preference is not simple. No one-to-one correlation between size and stealing preference exists. The original hypothesis, based on the usual assumptions concerning the effect of organizational size on attitudes, needs modification, even though a relationship between size of the victim organization and stealing preference is confirmed.

PUBLIC ATTITUDES TOWARD "CHISELING" WITH REFERENCE TO UNEMPLOYMENT COMPENSATION *

ERWIN O. SMIGEL

This study of attitudes toward the violation of unemployment compensation laws grew out of earlier research on unemployed veterans[1] and their use of, and attitudes toward, the Readjustment Allowance. Research in this area throws light on the unemployed worker and is, in addition, of continued interest to the student of social security.

The present paper also has implications for the criminologist and other investigators of social norms, since it is concerned with attitudes toward a type of criminal behavior more or less ignored

* American Sociological Review, Vol. 18, No. 1, February, 1953. Revision of a paper read at the annual meetings of the Ohio Valley Sociological Society, April 25, 1952. The research was supported by a grant from the Graduate School of Indiana University. Acknowledgment is due to Karl F. Schuessler and Albert K. Cohen for their numerous suggestions and to Mrs. Donald Auster for her help with the statistics.
[1] Henry J. Meyer and Erwin O. Smigel, "Job-Seeking and the Readjustment Allowance for Veterans," *American Journal of Sociology*, LVI (January, 1951), pp. 341–347.

until Sutherland,[2] Clinard,[3] Hartung,[4] and others began their studies of white collar crime. Acceptance of, or application for, unemployment compensation to which one is not entitled is considered crime by the criterion[5] that the violation of criminal law constitutes crime. This viewpoint implies that the behavior under discussion is regarded by the law[6] as socially harmful and that penalties[7] for such behavior are provided.

Although applying for or taking unemployment compensation illegally constitutes a crime (as defined) it is not "conventional" crime nor is it white collar crime.[8] In many ways, however, it is similar to white collar crime. Among the more important similarities are: (a) the participant is not professional—crime is not the way he regularly makes his living; (b) the individual does not conceive himself as a "criminal"; (c) furthermore, he is not usually regarded by the public as a "criminal"; (d) the criminal intent of the actor is sometimes in doubt and often difficult to determine; (e) the participant is not prosecuted as frequently as are those who commit "conventional" crimes; (f) the violation often involves manipulation of government regulations; and finally, (g) violations are often handled by administrative rather than judicial agencies.

[2] Edwin H. Sutherland, *White Collar Crime,* New York: The Dryden Press, 1949.
[3] Marshall B. Clinard, *The Black Market,* New York: Holt, Rinehart and Winston, 1952.
[4] Frank E. Hartung, "White Collar Offenses in the Wholesale Meat Industry in Detroit," *American Journal of Sociology,* LVI (July, 1950), pp. 25–32.
[5] Not all criminologists agree with this criterion. For some of the arguments, see: Paul Tappan, "Who Is the Criminal?" *American Sociological Review,* XII (February, 1947), pp. 96–102, and E. W. Burgess, "Discussion" of Hartung's article and Hartung's "Rejoinder," *op. cit.,* pp. 32–34.
[6] Indiana Employment Security Act (Effective April 1, 1947), Article XXV, Section 3602. This Act also provides for the compensation. In general, the provisions pertinent to an understanding of this study are: employers make financial contributions, employees do not; in order to be eligible for the compensation, the applicant must be able, willing and available for work; he must be out of work through no fault of his own (is disqualified from receiving benefits for six weeks if he has quit or been discharged for misconduct); must apply for suitable work and accept such suitable work when found for and offered to him (or be ineligible for benefits for six weeks) by the Indiana State Employment Service with which he must register.
[7] Sutherland, *op. cit.,* p. 31.
[8] For a discussion of criminal typing, see: A. R. Lindesmith and H. W. Dunham, "Some Principles of Criminal Typology," *Social Forces,* 19 (October–May, 1940–41), pp. 307–14.

The major factors which differentiate the type of crime discussed above from white collar crime are: (a) instances of this kind of violation can be found in any social class—not just the upper classes as in white collar crime; (b) the sum involved for each crime is generally much smaller than in white collar crime; and (c) the violation does not necessarily or usually grow directly out of the individual's occupation as it does in white collar crime. It should be noted that the type of crime discussed here is similar to "conventional" crime in the same three factors which differentiate it from white collar crime.

Many newspapers and popular magazines have shown interest in violations of the unemployment compensation laws and have called this behavior "chiseling." The label can tentatively be used for this subtype of the more inclusive area of crime described above, if chiseling is defined as implying an effort to get "something for nothing," which is recognized as generally being "against the law," but to which the ordinary connotations and stigma of "criminal" do not attach. It emphasizes the idea of shrewdly turning a situation to one's own advantage.

This study presents some information on public attitudes toward the violation of unemployment compensation[9] laws and perhaps has significance for the understanding of this relatively unexplored type of crime of which "chiseling" unemployment compensation from the state is only one sub-category. More specifically, the attempt is made here to: (a) describe and interpret some of the verbalized attitudes of non-transient[10] residents of Bloomington, Indiana, toward "chiseling" unemployment compensation from the government; (b) examine variations in these attitudes as related to the variety of situations presented and to the backgrounds of the respondents. Three major circumstances, often interrelated, appear to affect attitudinal responses with reference to infringements of the unemployment compensation laws: (1) Knowledge; *i.e.*, individuals who are familiar with the laws and regulations concerning unemployment compensation tend to have somewhat different attitudes toward the illegal application for, or acceptance of, unemployment compensation from those

[9] The terms "unemployment compensation" and "unemployment insurance" will be used interchangeably.
[10] Any adult who had lived in the city for at least seven months was considered non-transient.

who are not familiar with these provisions. (2) Social norms; *i.e.*, individuals who subscribe to differing social norms react, partially at least, on the basis of these norms. (3) Socio-economic factors; *i.e.*, individuals included in a particular social stratum tend to have somewhat different attitudes from persons in other social strata. This paper will revolve around these three circumstances.

A systematic random sample of 218 non-transient adults was obtained from the population list of the Bloomington City Directory.[11] All except six members of the sample who refused to participate in the study were interviewed in their homes. In addition to standard background questions and some specific queries to determine the degree of information concerning purpose and source of funds for the compensation, eight hypothetical situational questions were asked. The questions included a variety of the most usual circumstances involving "chiseling" the government of unemployment compensation, formulated from information provided by members of the local Employment Security Division. The respondent was given the choice[12] of expressing five differing degrees of approval toward each situation. All members of the sample submitted to a face-to-face interview which took from half an hour to two hours.

In addition, 31 individuals, randomly selected from the 218, were interviewed in detail. These respondents were requested to answer all the items the larger sample answered, and were then asked to explain their replies—with emphasis placed on the situational questions. An attempt was also made to get at attitudes and shades of attitudes which might not have been obtainable through the shorter schedule.

A significant finding of this study is that despite differential knowledge of the law, despite differences in social background, the majority of the sample disapproved [13] of "chiseling" the state

[11] *Polk's Bloomington (Monroe County, Indiana), City Directory 1950,* R. D. Polk and Company, St. Louis, Missouri.

[12] The interviewee had the following choices in Likert Scale Fashion: 1. Strongly approve, 2. Approve, 3. Indifferent, 4. Disapprove, 5. Strongly disapprove. The number to the left of each answer is the weight assigned to it and the sum of these responses constitutes the Unemployment Compensation scores which appear in the tables.

[13] Over the years there have been shifts in attitudes toward unemployment compensation regulations. Ralph Altman found that: "During low-level employment periods public opinion stands behind the 'easy' rule on availability

of unemployment compensation in all the different situations presented to them. Nevertheless, differences in attitudes do exist, and these variations will now be examined.

INFLUENCE OF KNOWLEDGE

One hypothesis designed to help explain the differentials in attitudes was that ignorance of the eligibility requirements of the law, ignorance of the purpose of the law, and ignorance of who pays for the benefits provided by the law affected the attitudes of the respondents to violations of that law. To collect some evidence on the effect of ignorance of the eligibility requirements on attitudes, two sets of situational questions were devised. Both dealt with illegal behavior toward those portions of the Indiana Employment Security Act which are concerned with eligibility for unemployment compensation. One set, composed of three situational questions, each covering a different type of illegal circumstance, was given the interviewee without telling him that they involved transgressions of the law. Then a second set of three questions was designed by rewriting the situations which made up the first set. These paired questions covered the same illegalities but were presented in a somewhat different context. The second set of situations was given to the same respondent after he was told: "The following situations all involve illegal action; however, many people may not agree with the law and feel that the individuals concerned are justified, in these instances, in breaking it."

To test the equivalence of these three paired situations, the six questions which make up the paired situations were given to a group of 116 Indiana University students. Two forms of these same six questions were distributed alternately among the students; one form stated that the behavior described in all six situations was illegal, the other form said nothing about the six situations being illegal. The respondents had an opportunity of

and is offended by stringent policies of inquiry into the availability for work of the unemployed. . . . As business improves and unemployment recedes, the availability changes. Claimants are 'choosier' and unemployment compensation authorities are more careful. They challenge and test the availability of more and more applicants for benefits. . . . And public opinion applauds this." *Availability for Work,* Cambridge, Massachusetts: Harvard University Press, 1950, p. 4.

answering the questions from a choice of five answers ranging from strongly disapprove to strongly approve. The arithmetic means of the responses to paired situation 1 were almost identical for both forms, as were those to paired situation 2; the means of responses to paired situation 3 were not. For example, the arithmetic means for the situations where illegality was not specifically stated were 3.9 for situation 1 and its equivalent situation 1a, 3.3 for situation 2 and its equivalent situation 2a, but 4.5 for situation 3 and 3.4 for its paired situation 3a. A similar relationship existed for the six circumstances where illegality was known. These figures indicated that the situations making up paired situation 1 and those composing paired situation 2 were closely equivalent, while those comprising paired situation 3 were not.

Most of the 212 persons in the Bloomington sample disapproved of the behavior described in the situations before they were told that the action was illegal. Some of this disapproval might have been expected, since even before being informed that a situation is illegal, many people can be presumed to know that it is illegal.

Table 1 indicates that for paired situation 1 [14] some slight tendency toward greater disapproval existed after the respondents were informed of the illegality of the situations. However, when the interviewees were told of the illegality in the second portion of paired situation 2, there was a statistically significant shift in the direction of disapproval. In these situations involving sick-

[14] The exact wording for one situation from each of the three paired situations reads:

(1) John Smith had worked for three years in a large plant; tiring of his job, he quit. Six weeks later, when eligible, he applied for unemployment insurance. However, while receiving unemployment insurance, he earned some money doing odd jobs which he did not report.

(2) Dan Smith left his job because of ill health. After six weeks when able to go to the State Employment Service, he applied for unemployment insurance, saying he was well enough to work, when actually he wasn't quite ready for work.

(3) Jack Green decided to quit his job and take a rest he felt he needed. The boss was a friend of his and gave him a slip saying he had been laid off. Jack took the slip and applied for unemployment insurance which was given him.

Interested readers may obtain from the author the four other situations which were used in this investigation but which do not appear verbatim in this paper.

Table 1

Attitudes of Respondents Toward Infractions of UC Laws Before and After Being Informed of the Illegality of the Situation

Principle of the Paired Situation[1]	attitudes[2]	Not Informed of Illegality		Informed of Illegality	
		number	per cent	number	per cent
1 Unemployed, applied	Approved	27	12.7	23	10.9
for and received UC;	Indifferent	33	15.6	34	16.0
earned additional	Disapproved	152	71.7	155	73.1
money through self-	Total	212	100.0	212	100.0
employment but did not report it.		Chi square = .4, P more than .8			
2 Ill, unable to work;	Approved	53	25.0	44	20.7
applied for UC.	Indifferent	56	26.4	33	15.6
	Disapproved	103	48.6	135	63.7
	Total	212	100.0	212	100.0
		Chi square = 11.2, P less than .01			
3 Collusion to show	Approved	15	7.1	24	11.3
eligibility for UC.	Indifferent	19	9.0	34	16.0
	Disapproved	178	83.9	154	72.7
	Total	212	100.0	212	100.0
		Chi square = 8.1, P between .01 and .02			

1 Each paired situation is made up of two situations designed to be equivalent, though paired situation 3 proved not to be.
2 All degrees of approval replies were combined, as were all degrees of disapproval.

ness, the respondents had less previous knowledge that a violation had occurred than in the first situations involving self-employment. This lack of knowledge may help account for differences in change to disapproval between paired situation 1 and 2, when knowledge of illegality was added. Paired situation 3, however, leaned in the opposite direction. There seemed to be a number of reasons for this. Collusion was obvious; therefore the interviewee had more previous knowledge than in the other paired situations that the described behavior was illegal. In addition, the independent test of the equivalence of the paired situations revealed that the conditions of paired situation 3 were not equivalent. This lack of equivalence plus easily recognizable il-

legality were biasing factors and probably explain why the results for paired situation 3 ran counter to those found in the
other paired situations.

For paired situations 1 and 2, where shifts in attitudes occurred between inclusive attitudinal categories (*i.e.*, changes from
approval to disapproval or indifference or changes in the reverse
direction, or shifts from indifference to disapproval or approval),
there was, as expected, a considerably greater percentage shift
toward disapproving the illegal action than toward approving it
when the individual was informed of the situation's illegality.

While the statistics are not conclusive, evidence is available
from the detailed interviews that a portion of the change from
approval to disapproval is due to the knowledge of the illegality
involved in the situation. For some, at least, the law seems to
act as a guide. As one schoolteacher pointed out, "The plan can
only work if everything is adhered to—if the intention of the
law is disobeyed—it's wrong." Or, as an assembler put it, "If it's
illegal—why then it's illegal."

It was thought that ignorance of who pays for the insurance
was related to "chiseling" unemployment compensation from the
government. While 82 per cent of the sample did not know who
paid for the compensation, the more significant figure is that
69 per cent thought the worker paid or partially paid for his own
benefit. These people not only did not know who paid for unemployment insurance but "knew" incorrectly. Most of these
individuals confused unemployment compensation with Old-Age
and Survivors Insurance to which the employee does contribute.[15]
Ten per cent of the sample who knowingly approved of illegal
application for, or receipt of, unemployment compensation also
thought the worker paid all or part of his benefit. The point of
view of these people is that the employee buys at least a part of
his own insurance and he should therefore be allowed to with-
draw the money he put in for that protection. These individuals
generally place few stipulations on the conditions of unemployment. One respondent said that the illegal behavior involving
collusion was "All right; after all they both [employer and

[15] A similar confusion was found among the residents of Elmira, New York.
John W. McConnell and Robert Risley, *Economic Security*, Ithaca, New
York: New York State School of Industrial and Labor Relations, Cornell
University, 1951, Bulletin 18, p. 19.

employee] put the money in. Why shouldn't they take it out if they agree?" Another individual was indifferent toward the illegal action described in a second situation because "Half of what he's taking is his own money." In general, those who thought the worker paid, or partially paid, for his own compensation and who approved of the illegal behavior did so because "He's only drawing some of what he paid in."

When given an opportunity to pick the main purpose of unemployment compensation from five possible answers, 52 per cent of the respondents chose correctly. It had been hypothesized that a relationship existed between not knowing the purpose of the compensation and a lenient attitude toward illegal acceptance of unemployment insurance. No statistical correlation was found.

However, statements made by the respondents, such as, "If he's sick he should have insurance—especially since he pays part of it," suggest a possible connection between source and purpose. The following figures indicate the strength of this connection: 58 per cent of those who knew the source of money for unemployment compensation also knew the purpose; 55 per cent of those who did not know the source did not know the purpose. To determine the relationship between a combination of these two factors and attitudes toward infringements of unemployment compensation laws, an index made up of five degrees of knowledge of source and purpose was designed, and the answers of the respondents ranked. The rankings were then cross-tabulated with the responses to the situations before the interviewees were informed of the illegality of the situation. The results suggest that those respondents who strongly disapproved may have been influenced by their accurate knowledge of source and purpose; however, for the other degrees of approval knowledge or lack of it seem to have no effect.

While the statistical evidence to support the hypothesis that ignorance of the law affects attitudes toward transgressions of that law has not been strong, the non-statistical evidence strongly points out that knowledge of the law does play a part in determining attitudes[16] toward violations of that law. Some individuals who approved of the illegal behavior did so because they were

[16] See: Milton Oman and Richard Tomasson, "Disparities in Visualizing Social Norms," *Social Forces*, 3 (March, 1952), pp. 328–333.

ignorant of the law and unaware that violations of the law were involved.

INFLUENCE OF SOCIAL NORMS

There are strong indications that social norms or values also have an effect on attitudes toward "chiseling." The arithmetic means for each situation, as shown in Table 2, reflect the differ-

Table 2
Arithmetic Means and Standard Deviations of Scores for Attitudes Toward Infractions of UC Laws by Paired Situations

Paired Situations[1]	Not Informed of Illegality		Informed of Illegality	
	mean[2]	standard deviation	mean	standard deviation
1	3.75	.87	3.83	.86
2	3.26	1.00	3.56	1.01
3	4.15	.89	3.85	.92

1 See Table 1 for principles of paired situations.
2 Possible scores range from 1 through 5.

ences in attitudes toward "chiseling"—the lower the mean, the greater the approval of the illegal behavior; the higher the mean, the less the approval of the behavior.

The lowest means involved situations which dealt with the acceptance of unemployment compensation when the worker was sick. The scores suggest that this behavior is more acceptable than "chiseling" in other situations because, as the interviews reveal, many of the respondents feel that the sick should be helped. For example, when asked whether or not sick people who were unemployed should be covered by the Indiana Employment Security Act, the majority, 60 per cent, approved such coverage. They expressed their favorable attitudes in this fashion: "A man in ill health should get it." Or, "He needs it more than anyone else." And, "Someone has to take care of the sick worker."

The social norms centering around the desire to help the sick seem, for those who approve of the illegal behavior, stronger than the conflicting norms centering around breaking the law. This conclusion is suggested in Table 2, for even though more respondents shifted their attitude toward disapproval when informed that acceptance of unemployment compensation when sick was illegal, more also reacted favorably to the violation in paired situation 2 than they did in the others. For some of those who continued to approve, these mores involving aid to the sick tend to outweigh the legality.

While situations concerning sickness met with the most approval, situations where the conflict between norms is not so great and where the illegality is more apparent met with the least. This attitude is reflected in the detailed interviews, especially for the incidents involving collusion. Many respondents strongly disapproved of this behavior. One said, "It's going around the law—pull." Another suggested, "Might have been a lot of people who felt the same way but couldn't get by with it." And a third remarked, "Not right—boss was helping him out because he knew him." When the social norms and the laws agree, as they do in the situations involving collusion, the illegal behavior is often sharply disapproved.

Table 2 offers some additional evidence on this point. Where the norms are in strong conflict (care of the sick versus obedience to the law in situation 2) greater variability in attitudes, as reflected by the standard deviations, can be seen. When the norms are in agreement there seems to be a greater convergence in attitudes; when they are in conflict, there seems to be a greater divergence in attitudes.

Complicating matters somewhat is the fact that norms generally thought to be in conflict are often found to be compatible. This is especially so for the social norms involved in the following situation:[17]

Fred Gordon was laid off. He applied for unemployment compensation to which he was entitled. About a week later when he went to the state employment service, they sent him to a job similar to the one he had just left. Fred had decided to look for a better job. However, to stay eligible for unemployment insurance he had to apply for the job offered him. When interviewed

[17] Technically, the illegality of the behavior described in this situation is open to question. This should have little effect on the verbalized attitudes of the respondents, for: (1) a technical interpretation of the law is involved; (2) the intent to circumvent the law is clear; and (3) the interviewees were informed that the behavior was illegal.

for the job he acted in such a way that he was not hired. He continued to receive unemployment insurance.

The norms considered in conflict in the above situation are those which advocate the "get-ahead" or upward mobility values versus "honesty is the best policy." Seventy-three per cent of the sample disapproved of the behavior described in the situation above after being informed of its illegality. What proportion of those who disapproved found these values in conflict and what proportion found them compatible is not known. Those who believe the two concepts compatible recognized the group norms of getting ahead—but within the rules. As one storekeeper said, "It's dishonest, he's not complying with the spirit of the law; and what's more he should work and look." Or, as a housewife remarked, "He took advantage—he should have taken the job and looked afterwards." A third simply said, "He should look on his own time."

For some of the 27 per cent who approved of, or were indifferent toward, the illegal behavior described in the situation, getting ahead seems more important than "Thou shalt not steal." For many of those who approve of the behavior the social norms may be in conflict. One woman said, "He should have a chance to better himself." Another approving respondent stated, "The man had ambition to get another job." For some who were indifferent, the norms were more evenly balanced: "Legally not right—but morally right—a guy has to look after himself a little bit." Another person who was indifferent said, "I hate to condemn a man for trying to better himself." The type of information reported here suggests the need for further research on the comparative influence of conflicting norms on attitudes and behavior.

INFLUENCE OF SOCIO-ECONOMIC FACTORS

Occupation, education, socio-economic status (SES), and other socio-economic factors are correlated with attitudes toward violations of the unemployment compensation laws. While these are not entirely separate from the preceding elements which make for differential attitudes, they are important and in harmony with what is known about a person's place in a community and his forms of behavior.

Table 3

Relation Between Occupation and Attitudes Toward Infractions of UC Laws

	UC Score[2]						
	11–15 Approve to Indifferent		16–20 Indifferent to Disapprove		21–25 Disapprove to Strongly Disapprove		Total	
Counts' Occupation Scale[1]	num- ber	per cent	num- ber	per cent	num- ber	per cent	num- ber	per cent
1 Higher business and higher professional	0	0	15	58	11	42	26	100
2 Lower business and lower professional	4	9	28	62	13	29	45	100
3 Better clerical and skilled	6	13	30	64	11	23	47	100
4 Lower clerical and skilled	6	14	32	74	5	12	43	100
5 Semi-skilled	4	15	21	81	1	4	26	100
6 Laborers— service workers	4	20	14	70	2	10	20	100
Unknown	2		1		2		5	
Total	26	12	141	67	45	21	212	100

Chi square[3] = 17.1, P less than .01.

1 Adaptation of Counts' Scale of Occupations. Genevieve Knupfer, Indices, of Socio-Economic Status, New York, 1946, p. 182.
2 See footnote 12.
3 In applying the chi square test to Table 3, adjacent cell frequencies were combined as needed to insure that each frequency would meet minimum cell requirements. Also, respondents whose occupation was unknown were omitted in this analysis. These modifications resulted in a 3 by 3 table.

Respondents in this survey who have poor jobs and low socio-economic statuses are more inclined to approve of "chiseling" unemployment compensation from the government, whereas those who are more educated, have good jobs and high socio-economic statuses more strongly disapprove the illegal behavior.

Attitudes toward "chiseling" unemployment compensation from the state are clearly affected by the person's occupational level. Persons lower in the occupational scale are more inclined to approve of "chiseling." These findings for attitudes toward infractions of the unemployment compensation laws agree with Centers' conclusions regarding the correlation between occupation and attitudes.

The lowest occupational ranks, *i.e.*, the semi-skilled and unskilled workers, represent the frontier of one direction in attitude and behavior, the top business group represents the extreme in another. Unanimity of opinion within either stratum is not admittedly the rule. . . .[18]

What was revealed for occupation was in general found for education and socio-economic status—see Tables 4 and 5. For

Table 4
Relation Between Education and Attitudes Toward Infractions of UC Laws

	UC Score							
	11–15 Approve to Indifferent		16–20 Indifferent to Disapprove		21–25 Disapprove to Strongly Disapprove		Total	
Years of Schooling	num-ber	per cent	num-ber	per cent	num-ber	per cent	num-ber	per cent
8 or less	7	14.3	34	69.4	8	16.3	49	100
9–12	10	11.6	60	69.8	16	18.6	86	100
13–16	9	17.0	33	62.3	11	20.7	53	100
Over 16	0	0	14	58.3	10	41.7	24	100
Total	26	12	141	67	45	21	212	100

Chi square[1] $= 3.1$, P more than .5.

1 In applying the chi square test to Table 4, adjacent cell frequencies were combined as needed to insure that each frequency would meet minimum cell requirements. This modification resulted in a 3 by 3 table.

example, those individuals with a socio-economic status of A were the most disapproving, those with a socio-economic status of D the most approving.

While Table 4 does show that the higher the socio-economic

[18] Richard Centers, *The Psychology of Social Classes*, Princeton, New Jersey: Princeton University Press, 1949, p. 108.

Table 5
Relation Between SES and Attitudes Toward Infractions of UC Laws

	UC Score							
	11–15 Approve to Indifferent		16–20 Indifferent to Disapprove		21–25 Disapprove to Strongly Disapprove		Total	
SES[1]	num- ber	per cent	num- ber	per cent	num- ber	per cent	num- ber	per cent
A	0	0	5	62.5	3	37.5	8	100
B	4	7.0	36	65.0	15	28.0	54	100
C	16	14.0	75	65.0	24	21.0	115	100
D	6	19.3	23	74.2	2	6.5	31	100
Unknown			3		1		4	
Total	26	12	141	67	45	21	212	100

Chi square[2] = 5.6, P between .05 and .10.

1   Adaptation of index designed by the Pulse of New York, Inc., Genevieve Knupfer, <u>Indices of Socio-Economic Status</u>, New York, 1946, p. 159.
2   In applying the chi square test to Table 5, adjacent cell frequencies were combined as needed to insure that each frequency would meet minimum cell requirements. Also, respondents whose SES was unknown were omitted in this analysis. These modifications resulted in a 3 by 2 table.

status, the less the approval of breaches of the unemployment compensation law, this probably does not indicate a greater morality on the part of the upper classes. Sutherland found that when opportunity was negligible the lower classes had a lower rate of some types of violation:

Variations among persons in the lower socio-economic class in the frequency of violations of particular laws may be similarly affected by their economic position. Unskilled laborers do not violate the anti-trust laws or commit fraud in advertising, because they are not in a position appropriate for such crimes. Negroes have a very low rate of embezzlement because they seldom occupy positions of financial trust.[19]

Similar factors seem to apply here for attitudes, but in reverse. In this study, individuals in the lower socio-economic

[19] Sutherland, *op. cit.*, p. 263.

status groupings were closer to the situation, while respondents in the upper social strata were not only further from the opportunity but were, for businessmen at least, on the other side of the fence. The Indiana Employment Security Act[20] provides for an increase or decrease in the tax employers pay toward the

Table 6
Relation Between Unemployment, Receiving UC or Government Aid and Attitudes Toward Infractions of UC Laws

	UC Score						
	11–15 Approve to Indifferent		16–20 Indifferent to Disapprove		21–25 Disapprove to Strongly Disapprove		Total
	number	per cent	number	per cent	number	per cent	number	per cent
Total	26	12	141	67	45	21	212	100
Unemployed within last ten years								
Yes	9	15	44	73	7	12	60	100
No	17	11	97	64	38	25	152	100
Chi square = 5.3, P between .10 and .05								
Received UC								
Yes	5	15	24	73	4	12	33	100
No	21	12	117	65	41	23	179	100
Chi square = 3.4, P more than .10								
Received government aid								
Yes	13	15.1	60	69.8	13	15.1	86	100
No	13	10.3	81	64.3	32	25.4	126	100
Chi square = 3.3, P more than .10								

benefit, varying with the amounts their employees draw. It is logical that employers should be among the most disapproving. Related to opportunity or closeness to the actual situation as a

[20] Indiana Employment Security Act, *op. cit.*, Article XI, Section 1103.

reason for differential atittudes are personal experiences with unemployment, with receiving economic aid from the government, and with applying for unemployment compensation. That is, those who have had these experiences were more approving; those who have not had these experiences were more disapproving.

The evidence tends to bear out the following hypothesis: the nearer the individual is to the situation, the greater the tendency to approve, or at least be indifferent toward, illegal behavior with reference to unemployment compensation.[21]

In general, while most respondents disapprove of "chiseling" the government of unemployment compensation, some variation in attitude does exist. These differences, which are probably due to a large number of variables, are more clearly affected, though this is not always indicated statistically, by three major interrelated factors: ignorance of the law, differing social norms, and differences in socio-economic status.

[21] A fourth factor which helps determine attitudinal responses, while not specifically discussed here, involves the effect of distinct personal experience and offers an exception to the hypothesis. An example of this type of experience may be observed in the remarks of a woman who said of the behavior described in one situation: "I don't see why he should get the insurance; my husband [under similar conditions] didn't."

BLUE-COLLAR THEFT: CONCEPTIONS OF PROPERTY, ATTITUDES TOWARD PILFERING, AND WORK GROUP NORMS IN A MODERN INDUSTRIAL PLANT

DONALD N. M. HORNING

Thefts by workers from their place of employment have been a source of concern to owners, managers, and labor representatives from the earliest beginnings of productive systems. More recently, they have become the onus of security officials, protection agencies, surety, bonding and insurance companies, as well as the numerous representatives of arbitration and grievance-handling agencies. This concern, however, has been largely of a pragmatic nature, focusing on the prevention, control, and regulation of theft in the plant. Thefts of this type, though constituting a significant financial loss to industry and presumably involving a significant proportion of industrial workers, have not been accorded much attention by either the students of deviant behavior or the analysts of complex bureaucracies. Even sociologists, with their empirical, analytical, and theoretical interest in normative behavior, have been conspicuously neglectful of the nonlegal activities of industrial operatives. In an attempt to bridge this hiatus, this report, which is derived from a more

46

comprehensive study of blue-collar theft,[1] focuses on the cognitive dimensions of pilfering—namely, the workers' conceptions of property in the plant, their attitudes toward pilfering, and the work groups' norms relative to pilfering.

Pilfering, peculation, filching, mulcting, poaching, embezzling, stealing, petty thievery, petty larceny and purloining are the terms used most often in describing the acts which are the focus of this inquiry. These terms, however, do not reveal the nature of the relationship between the thief and his victim: the act may be perpetrated by a person who has a viable relationship with the organization or by one who has no ostensible contact with the organization outside of its victimization. Furthermore, these terms do not reveal whether the act was committed for or against the organization—that is, whether the organization was the benefactor or the victim. Thus, a worker engaged in industrial espionage, or stealing secrets for his company, is not benefiting directly or personally by the commission of his crime. It may be noted at this point that the failure of Sutherland, and his students, to acknowledge these subtle distinctions relative to the victim has resulted in a conceptual mélange that has continued to give immeasurable difficulty. Logically, it would appear that the concept of white-collar crime should be reserved for acts committed by wage-earning employees in which the company of their employ is either the victim or the locale for the commission of an illegal act from which they personally benefit. The term corporate crime could then be applied to those crimes generally included under the white-collar crime designation, namely those committed by employees in the course of their employment and for which the company is the primary benefactor. It is in this conceptual framework that the distinction between the terms blue-collar crime and blue-collar theft is introduced.

Blue-collar crime, the more generic concept, embraces the whole array of illegal acts which are committed by nonsalaried workers and which involve the operative's place of employment either as the victim (*e.g.,* the theft of materials, the destruction of company property, the falsification of production records) or

[1] Donald N. M. Horning, *Blue-Collar Theft: A Sociological Inquiry of Pilfering by Industrial Workers* (to be published by College and University Press, New Haven, Connecticut).

as a contributory factor by providing the locus for the commission of an illegal act (*e.g.*, fighting on company property, the theft of personal property, gambling on company premises, the selling of obscene literature on company premises).

Blue-collar theft, one form of blue-collar crime, may be defined simply as the illegal or unauthorized utilization of facilities or removal and conversion to one's own use of company property or personal property located on the plant premises by nonsalaried personnel employed in the plant.

THE METHODS AND PROCEDURES

The data on which this report is based were obtained from intensive semistructured interviews with 88 male operatives of a large Midwest electronics assembly plant. This plant was chosen because it had components, materials, and equipment that were readily pilferable and of some utility outside of the plant. The subjects represented four different job classifications: assemblers, troubleshooters, repairmen, and mule (fork-lift) drivers. These four categories were chosen for several reasons. First, it was felt that research should include all departments in the plant to prevent the workers in a given department from feeling that an accusing finger was being pointed at their department or section. Second, the research design required the selection of workers representing different levels of access to pilferable goods and materials found in the plant. Third, the research design called for workers representing a wide range of task specialization to discern the effect which different degrees of component-related knowledge had upon the incidence and pattern of employee theft. The assemblers were chosen because they had high access but low knowledge (of utility); troubleshooters, high access and high knowledge; repairmen, moderate access and moderate knowledge; mule drivers, low access and low knowledge. A total of 106 names were chosen from a list of male operatives furnished by the union; of these, fourteen refused to cooperate (a refusal rate of 13.2%). All interviews were conducted at the worker's residence. No workers were contacted at the plant, and the company was in no way involved in the planning or execution of the research.

Owing to the researcher's awareness of the workers' sensitivity to the question of pilfering in the plant and given the researcher's need to establish and maintain a climate favorable to the study, several noteworthy research techniques were employed. First, the workers were interviewed in a carefully planned sequence based upon the union leaders' perceptions of the general informal social organization of each of the departments in the work organization. Prior to interviewing the workers in the sample, all of the opinion leaders, thus identified, were interviewed and given complete information regarding the nature of the research (including copies of all research instruments). Although a few of these opinion leaders were also in the sample, most were not. The remaining subjects were then interviewed in the sequence suggested by the opinion leaders' perceptions of the status differentials extant in the informed work group. (This was accomplished by giving them the names of all of the subjects who were in their department and asking them to rank the subjects by degrees of relative influence.) This technique was employed because it was assumed that the opinion leaders and subleaders in the informal organization would become the informal emissaries of the investigator. By placing them in a position of knowledgeability, it was further assumed that the opinion leaders would seek to enhance their informal leadership role by discussing the research with the workers in their department in advance of its becoming common knowledge. This tacit acknowledgment of their leadership role, thus allowed them to play the role of the informed insider. Lacking such foreknowledge, it was felt they would most probably reject the research categorically, as their means of role affirmation. A second technique, employed in the interest of creating and maintaining a more favorable research climate, was in the realm of rumor control, or more specifically, rumor intervention. Starting with the premise that research of this type is likely to generate numerous rumors throughout the plant, several opinion leaders were asked to assist the investigator in covertly manipulating the content of the informal communication system. The opinion leaders were to inform the investigator of all rumors they heard regarding the research (*e.g.*, This is a company-sponsored project and is the precursor to a general crackdown on pilfering) and, upon instruction, they were to serve the counteractive function of introducing information (rumors) into the system which neutralized the content of the original rumor. This technique proved helpful in keeping the system of rumors in balance so that a particular "rumor set" didn't become "fixed" in the workers' cognitive frame of reference, thus contaminating their responses or precluding their cooperation.

CONCEPTIONS OF PROPERTY IN THE PLANT

"Who owns the property? I ain't never thought about it much —let's see: Well, you don't mean the workers' own stuff like lunch buckets. . . . they's a lot of stuff that I don't know about —it don't seem to belong to nobody—it's just there and you can take it if you want—I suppose it's the Company's though cause you got to sneak it out—but the super he don't seem to care if you take it. There's some things you'd never take—the Company wouldn't like it—I mean like a machine or drill or completed TV set or even a Kinne tube." [2]

"If you want to look at the little parts as Company property then I guess you'd say Company property goes out of there. . . . They take tubes for their own sets . . . I don't think anybody would want any of the 'Company's property' and besides it's too big to take anyway."

"Most of it belongs to the Company—but there are some things that are furnished by the Company which ya might say we own—fur instance, I got me a little electric fan that I made from junk I found out there—I've got my name painted on it—and nobody better ever try and take it—it's mine—everybody has things like that—the Company furnishes them but they are ours —the other day they had a big fight near me cause one worker took another guy's stool—you see what I mean?"

"I bring home things that are of use to me but not to them— fur instance, the vendors will mix up the screws and you might get a few odd ones in the barrel . . . they ain't ———'s material. It came in with their material but it's not really theirs cause they didn't order it . . . It's not stealing from ——— and the vendor he don't want it, he don't know nothin about it."

"When you talk about Company property what do you mean— just everything? As far as I'm concerned there's a lot of things down there that you might say belonged to the Company cause they paid for 'em but we don't look at it that way cause they don't seem to care—we take what we want and don't worry

[2] All quotes are taken from the interview schedules.

about it—I ain't never thought about those things as Company property—It just don't seem like it is."

"I don't know about the tools—they tell us they belong to the Company but they don't seem to care about them—it's like this —a worker is on the job for several years—he's had tools and equipment checked out the whole time—he goes to check them in when he's transferred to another section and they don't even know he's got them—they've lost the sign-out card—they tell you to keep it or give it to somebody. So who do they belong to —huh?"

A careful perusal of the foregoing quotes reveals a subtle but important cognitive distinction. In responding to the questions pertaining to the theft of materials from the company, the workers continually alluded to three broad classes of property in the plant: company property, personal property, and property of uncertain ownership. The operational, if not actual, existence of three categories of property in the plant introduces a significant change in the traditional "dichotomous" conception of company property and personal property. This cognitive dissonance between the actual and the perceived forms of property may account, in part, for the failure of security forces in controlling and regulating the activities of the pilferer as well as the failure of researchers and practitioners alike to produce sound generalizations about this form of behavior.

Whether operating from a dichotomous or trichotomous conception of property in the plant, it may be noted that each category of property is perceived by the workers as consisting of a hard core of relatively distinct objects and materials about which there is little disagreement. Moving from this core centrifugally, the workers place other elements in the property complex with decreasing certainty of ownership (in the case of personal and company property) or nonownership (in the case of property of uncertain ownership). This configuration is depicted in Figure 1 with the perceived category of uncertain ownership superimposed upon the real categories of company and personal property. The personal and company property about which there is generally the least certainty (*e.g.*, scrap, broken parts, etc.) constitute the hard core of the uncertain ownership category.

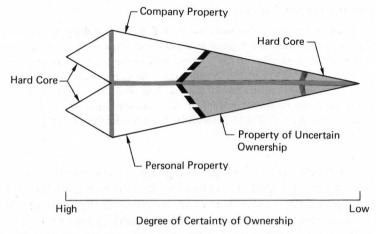

Figure 1   Degree of Certainty of Ownership by Type of Property

Viewed abstractly, the personal property in the plant is distinguishable from company property in that it consists of those objects which belong to specific individuals and which were purchased or produced by them at their own expense. When viewed from the workers' perspective, the boundaries are much more obscure, because personal property also includes certain forms of company property which the workers have appropriated for their own use; *e.g.* stools which have been modified for personal use; stool pads fabricated from packing material; "personal" items fabricated from junk parts; equipment on which safety devices or auxiliary devices have been attached, modified, or removed; and tools on which special grips have been added.

The hard core of personal property consists of all of the readily identifiable personal items which may be found in the plant—for example, marked or monogrammed clothing, lunch pails, inscribed jewelry, wallets, modified tools, specially adapted equipment and materials brought into the shop from the outside to be worked on for personal use. The items falling at the other end of the continuum where there is a low degree of certainty of ownership include unmarked clothing, money, jewelry, gloves and nonprescription safety goggles.

In addition to the building, fixtures, heavy machinery, and equipment, the hard core company property includes power tools, bulky and expensive components and any components, parts, materials, or tools which have a special value placed upon them by the company, such as those for which there is a checkout system or an established accounting procedure. For example, in the electronics plant under study, the components constituting the hard core of company property included: Kinne tubes (TV picture tubes), TV chassis, TV power transformers, TV masks (picture tube frames), reels of copper wire, TV tuners, pneumatic hand tools, electric drills, and portable testing equipment. The company property which had a low degree of certainty of ownership consists of the numerous materials, components, and tools which are small, plentiful, inexpensive, and expendable. This includes items such as nails, screws, sandpaper, nuts, bolts, scrap metal, wipe rags, scrap wood, electrical tape, solder, small production components (small TV tubes, resistors, capacitors, condensers, knobs, dial shafts) and small tools (ceramic adjusting tools, pliers, screwdrivers, drill bits and wrenches).

As shown in Figure 1, the category designated as property of uncertain ownership actually consists of those items of personal and company property for which legitimate proprietary claims may be made but which lie at the low degree of certainty of ownership end of the continuum. In practice, however, the workers view this as a separate category consisting of those items about which they have serious doubts concerning ownership. Thus, the items at the low degree of certainty end of the corporate ownership continuum (*e.g.*, screws, nails, nuts, bolts, scraps, waste, and certain types of tools) are viewed as not belonging to anyone. Similarly, personal items, such as lost money, a stray[3] item of clothing or equipment, are viewed as not having an owner. The hard core of the uncertain category actually consists of those items about which there is a legitimate question of ownership: scrap and waste material; nonreturnable, broken, or defective components; broken tools, etc. For example, when a screwdriver, furnished by the company, has been ground down to the point where it is too short to use and the company has the worker turn it in only to throw it away, to whom does the screwdriver belong once it has been placed in the scrap barrel? To take another example from the company under study, when one assembler received the components he was to work with, they were wrapped

[3] Not at an assigned work station or within a given worker's territory.

in a protective material which was held in place with a rubber band. The rubber bands were not salvaged; they were considered scrap by the company. To whom do they belong? Figure 1 depicts the uncertain ownership category as tapering off as one approaches the definable ownership end of the continuum. It is depicted as extending along the continuum, however, because there are occasions where the company (or individual) is viewed as having relinquished a legitimate claim of ownership through default, *e.g.*, a power tool which has been replaced by newer equipment and which has not been recalled. In every respect—legal, moral, theoretical—the object is still company property, but in the worker's view it has, by default, slipped into the limbo of property of uncertain ownership.

To complete the picture of the worker's conceptions of property in the plant, several additional observations may be noted. First, the items which fall at a particular point on the continuum do not necessarily remain fixed at that point. An item, or a class of items, may shift from the low degree of certainty end of the continuum to the high degree of certainty of ownership as conditions change. For example, in the electronics plant, solenium rectifiers were originally considered by the workers as falling within the uncertain ownership category. They were available in large quantity, were not subject to special inventory, were generally available throughout the plant and were simply discarded if defective. However, when the company introduced a loose system of control by requiring the workers to check out the quantities needed for production, the rectifiers were immediately perceived differently by the workers as they were shifted to the hard core company-property category. Second, the scope of the uncertain ownership category appears to be inversely related to the extent to which management regulates the flow of goods and materials within the plant. Thus a high degree of control, such as that which might be found in the research and development section (where there is constant danger of industrial espionage and pirating and where even the scrap may be considered classified), most probably results in a very small residual of items in the uncertain ownership category. According to several old-timers, when the electronics plant was under wartime security, the things that were regarded as of uncertain ownership "were about nil."

WORKERS' ATTITUDES TOWARD PILFERING PROPERTY IN THE PLANT

"People have a different attitude toward the Company than they do toward each other or you. . . . They wouldn't come into your home and take thirty cents, but they will take from the Company. They figure it's got plenty of money and a few cents don't mean nothing to them . . . but for you they figure there's not so much of it.[4]

"Occasionally I'll bring something home accidentally. I'll stick it in my pocket and forget it and bring it home. I don't return those cause it's only a small part and I didn't take it intentionally."

"It's a corporation . . . It's not like taking from one person . . . the people justify it that the corporation wouldn't be hurt by it . . . they just jack the price up and screw the customer. They're not losing anything. The Company told us that last year they lost $30,000 . . . but that was for losses of all types. It gives them a nice big tax write-off. I'll bet you a goddamm day's pay that they jack that son-of-a-bitchin' write-off way up too."

"There are several things involved . . . in the first place I work with those little bastards [tubes] all day and I have come to regard them as worthless and besides the Company gets 'em for practically nothing. But if I go out and buy them then the cost is terrible. The markup on the stuff is like drugs . . . it's very, very high. They've got plenty . . . they're not losing anything on what I take."

"Many of the workers feel that they are part of the Company and so they might not feel as guilty because they're taking from themselves."

"Never heard of anybody stealing anything from others. That's one thing. You can leave something laying around down there and no one will risk their job for taking things from others. They would be more severe on you if they caught you taking things from the workers than if you were taking from the Company. The people seem to realize most workers are rather poor and couldn't afford to lose something. A Company won't miss it like a person would. This don't make it right but it justifies it in their mind."

[4] All quotes are taken from the interview schedules.

"They wouldn't think of stealing from one another: they may take tools but that's a special case because they don't consider that stealing from the worker—cause the Company gives 'em to the worker."

"I don't like the word *taken*. It's not like I was stealing those screws. They're not worth anything."

"When I look at the waste and breakage I don't feel at all guilty about it. I work with the parts all day. I have a supply right before me. I see so many broken and wasted they aren't of any value to me anymore. I have them around me all day and I don't regard them as worth much. When you are working for someone you can't see . . . I think you're more likely to not feel guilty. _____ is just a building—it doesn't mean anything to me except it's a place where I work. I don't mean nothing to them. Old man _____ doesn't know me from nobody and he doesn't care what happens to me, just so I don't foul up production."

"It's like this—if I needed a pot full of dirt for a little plant that I have and was driving along in the country and I saw this thousand-acre farm with nice dirt, I wouldn't ask the farmer for it. He'd think I was nuts. He'd probably say—'take a truckload'—sounds kind of silly don't it to ask for a pot of dirt with all that dirt there—the parts in the plant are the same. What's a little tube to——? They've got millions of them."

"Not as a rule they don't feel guilty. I know I don't—some may have guilt feelings—some may get neurotic over it but I don't. A good theoretical question is—'Is this theft?' I don't know what the answer would be though. I think that if it's for personal use it isn't but if it's for sale then it is theft."

"I heard of a guy who offered to pay someone to take some parts out for him because it was against his religion—now I think that's really low."

"I'm sure that I could go quite high in the upper supervision and get help in finding parts—they're quite helpful as long as it's for personal use. Well, you can't feel very guilty when you know even the supers approve."

The real significance of the trichotomous conception of property becomes apparent when one examines the workers' attitudes toward pilfering. Although the workers perceived three categories of property, they perceived only two victims: the company, in the case of company property and the individual, in the case of personal property. As might be expected in such a cognitive orientation, the property of uncertain ownership has no victim.

Given a tripartite conception of property and given a victim category extending from highly visible, specific individuals to nonvisible, vaguely conceptualized collectivities of stockholders, it is reasonable to expect that there is not a single attitude toward pilfering in the plant, but rather a complex configuration of attitudes specific to each property category and perceived victim. The viability of this conceptualization has already been established in Smigel's research on the shifting attitudes toward stealing as the organizational frame of reference is changed.[5] The present research suggests that these vacillating cognitive orientations also apply to pilfering in the work plant.

Insight into the workers' attitudes toward the pilfering of personal property may be obtained from an analysis of their conception of the relative frequency with which personal property is pilfered as well as their impression of the conditions under which it is likely to occur. Of the 88 subjects in the sample, only one believed that the pilfering of personal property was a frequent occurrence. The remaining 87 (99%) believed it occurred rarely or never. The workers who believed that it occurred rarely gave further insight into the workers' attitudes when they sought to explain their answers. Generally, their answers revealed that the pilfering of personal property which did occur was confined to property falling at the low degree of certainty end of the ownership continuum. When asked to explain the seemingly low incidence of pilfering of personal property, two basic responses were given. The majority of the workers responded by saying, "It just isn't done." Implied in this statement is the suggestion that a strong normative restraint, bordering on a taboo, exists in that its occurrence is unthinkable and thus does not need further explanation or rationale. The remaining workers gave replies which suggested that the visibility of the victim serves as an effective deterrent to the theft of personal property.

When asked to indicate whether they regarded the theft of personal or company property as the more serious form of theft,

[5] Erwin O. Smigel, "Public Attitudes Toward Stealing as Related to the Size of the Victim Organization," *American Sociological Review*, Vol. 21, No. 3, June 1956, pp. 320–327.

80% of the workers indicated that they regarded the theft of personal property as the more serious act. The remaining workers indicated they viewed both types of pilfering with equal gravity. None of the workers regarded theft from the company as a more serious act.

The feelings about pilfering of company property do not evoke nearly the consensus that there was on personal property. However, there is still a general pattern with almost four-fifths (78.4%), or 69, of the subjects indicating that it was wrong to take company property. Seven reported they thought it was not wrong, and twelve were uncertain. In explaining their replies, almost one-half (47.7%), or 42, of the subjects viewed the pilfering of company property as wrong because it violated the religico-moral code. They gave answers such as "It's a sin" and "God holds us accountable for all our acts" or "It's just wrong; that's all I know." Twenty-seven of those who felt it was wrong to take company property invoked a legalistic rationale with statements such as "It's against the law" or "Legally, it's wrong." The twelve workers who were uncertain generally made statements which implied the existence of a situational ethic in which the question of right or wrong could not be answered in the abstract; it depended wholly upon the circumstances attending the pilfering. Of the seven who indicated that the theft of company property was not wrong, the majority indicated that the taking of company property was not theft.

The attitudes toward the residual category of uncertain ownership was another matter. Here we begin to see a real disengagement from the traditional religious, moral, and legal restraints. Though the semantic shift was a subtle one of changing the line of questioning from the "taking of company property" to the "taking of things from the plant," the conceptual shift was very real.

Since it seems reasonable to assume that the workers' attitudes are, at least in part, a function of the perceived attitudinal milieu in the plant, the workers were asked to describe their fellow workers' feelings about the "taking of things" from the plant. Of the 88 subjects, 72 (81.8%) believed their peers do not feel guilty about their pilfering. Only fourteen workers reported their peers felt some guilt and two evaded the issue by indicating that they doubted if their peers ever took anything except on extremely rare occasions. The workers' explanations for their peers' feelings are even more illuminating in that they provide a window through which we may view the attitudinal milieu in the plant. These responses, which were classifiable into a number of themes, are presented in Table 1.

Table 1

Workers' Explanations for Their Peers' Feelings of Guilt or Failure to Feel Guilt After Removing Goods from the Company Premises (n=86)

	No. of responses	No. of subjects	% of total	% of responses in category
Reasons for feeling guilty		14	16	100
1 conscience-centered theme[a]	11		(13)	(79)
2 situation-centered theme[b]	3		(3)	(21)
Reasons for _not_ feeling guilty		72	84	100
1 don't regard as theft[c]	29	(29)	(34)	(40)
2 rationalized theft	43	(43)	(50)	(60)
a plant lore theme[d]	(19)			
b personal theme[e]	(9)			
c managerial theme[f]	(8)			
d economic theme[g]	(7)			

(Note: the numbers in parentheses are subtotals)

a   Conscience-centered theme: includes statements which bear some reference to the interplay of conscience in determining guilt, e.g., "We're on the honor system down there so the only thing to prevent theft is their conscience" or "It's wrong and they know it."

b   Situation-centered theme: includes statements referring to some aspect of the situation which serves as the precipitant of the guilt feeling and not necessarily the act itself, e.g., "feel guilty cause they don't need it" or "feel guilty cause they're taking more than they need."

c   Don't regard it as theft theme: includes statements which convey the notion that these acts do not constitute theft but are instead entirely acceptable, e.g., "They feel justified cause it's their company"; "it's part of the compensation for working there."

d   Plant lore theme: comprised of statements which are obviously among the sets of beliefs and notions that are carried along as part of the work groups' normative rationalizations, e.g., "The company doesn't mind if it's for personal use"; "Management doesn't mind if it's small parts" or "The company expects it."

e   Personal theme: comprised of statements in which reference is made to specific attributes of the pilferers, e.g., "They do it out of habit and so don't even think about it" and "It's the daredevil in us—the urge to gamble."

f   Managerial theme: made up of statements in which managerial acts and precedents are used as the point of departure for justifying their own acts, e.g., "We see managers doing it and what's good enough for them is good enough for us" or "Bosses will help us get stuff so how can it be wrong?"

g   Economic theme: in these, reference is made to the fact that the acts of pilfering serve the workers' ends as well as those of the company by saving them money, e.g., "Figure they're saving the company money by taking stuff they would have to throw away anyway."

Of the 88 subjects in the sample, 80 (91%) reported they had pilfered goods from the plant. However, not all of these were reported as being intentional; six workers reported their pilfering had consisted of the inadvertent removal of property from the plant, *e.g.,* "I got home and found I had a pocket full of screws which I had placed there and forgot." Of the 80 subjects who had pilfered, only one-third (36%) reported that they felt guilty while two-thirds (64%) reported that they did not feel guilty. The explanation for their feelings, though classifiable under many of the same general headings as those of their peers, reveal some notable differences. Table 2 classifies the workers' own explanations for their feelings about their pilfering.

Table 2

Workers' Explanations for Their Own Feelings of Guilt or Failure to Feel Guilt Arising from the Removal of Goods from the Company Premises (n=80)

	No. of responses	No. of subjects	% of total	% of responses in category
Reasons for feeling guilty		29[a]	36	100
1 conscience-centered theme	11			38
2 situation-centered theme	13			45
3 moral-centered theme[b]	14			48
Reasons for *not* feeling guilty		51	64	100
1 don't regard as theft	38	(38)		75
2 rationalized theft	13	(13)		25
a plant lore theme	9			
b personal theme	2			
c managerial theme	4			
d economic theme	2			

a The subtotals are greater than the number of respondents owing to the fact that some respondents gave answers which fell into several response categories, e.g., managerial and economic.
b Moral-centered theme: e.g., "It's a sin," and "It's against God's law."

A comparison of the data in Tables 1 and 2 reveals several interesting observations. First, in comparing the data relative to the assumptions about their peers' guilt and their own feelings, it appears that the workers are far more likely to ascribe guilt feelings to themselves (36%) than they are to others (16%). This suggests that though the normative system of the work subculture may provide the means for neutralizing acts of pilfering, thereby allowing the workers to assume their peers do not feel guilty, the workers themselves may have difficulty resolving the conflict between their work norms and the general societal norms. Secondly, it is interesting to note that of those who report they do not have feelings of guilt, the majority simply do not define their pilfering as theft. The pervasiveness of this desire to avoid labeling their acts as theft is also reflected in a number of the rationalizations which were proffered, *e.g.*, "The Company expects it" or "The Company doesn't mind."

Additional insight into the workers' attitudes toward pilfering may be obtained from their responses to the questions pertaining to the giving away and/or selling of goods and materials taken from the plant. Although about one-fourth of the 88 subjects admitted they had given goods away, only five reported they had sold pilfered goods. Almost all agreed that these acts were questionable, if not wrong. The taboo against the selling of pilfered goods appears particularly strong. Most workers indicated that the work group would not attempt to protect or cover up for the worker who was removing goods which he intended to sell.

THE WORK GROUP NORMS GOVERNING PILFERING IN THE WORK PLANT

"There's a guy on our line who's supposed to take things all the time. They tease him a lot—he really gets it when the line goes down because of a shortage of parts. They all start saying to him 'Hey, how about bringing in some of your parts so we can work tomorrow.' I don't know if this is just bullshit or not." [6]

"I've heard of three cases where people were caught. Two who were stealing and selling were fired outright. Another was given an involuntary quit. He was asked to quit. He refused so he was fired."

"What happens if you're caught—it depends upon the item. You're fired if its large—warned if it's small. Their policy seems to point to large quantity or high value. If you take often and are caught you're fired. If you do it only occasionally, then you are just warned."

[6] All quotes are taken from the interview schedules.

"Not when the taking is on a personal use basis. It's a generally accepted practice. Everybody is doing it so why should anyone feel guilty? The workers frown on people who do it on a large scale cause they're afraid the Company will crack down on everyone. When the big operators are caught everybody feels better but they won't turn him in. That's in a way kinda funny, isn't it? If he's fired they don't feel sorry for him. He gets what he deserves."

Since attitudes do not exist in a cultural vacuum, the preceding analysis has borne the tacit assumption that the work group subculture includes a set of norms which prescribe the types of property which are pilferable, the conditions under which pilfering should occur, as well as the conditions under which the workers can expect the tacit, if not overt, support of the work group.

The workers in the sample confirmed this assumption. The mechanisms through which these norms are conveyed to the workers appear, for the most part, to be in the form of folktales about heroes and recreants. These folktales consist of a congeries of episodes about pilferers—each tale bearing its own message. For example, the description of an unacceptable *modus operandi* can be a tale describing the types of materials for which workers have been discharged or reprimanded when they attempted to remove them from the plant, or a description of the ways in which the work group will cover up for a pilferer.

As might be expected, the work group norms do not delineate specifically what constitutes a reasonable amount of pilfering (*i.e.*, when one is not exceeding the tolerable limit). However, the norms do provide two broad guidelines for the pilferer. The first sets the limit by indicating that pilfering should be confined to the "valueless" property of uncertain ownership. The second indicates that pilfering should be limited to that which is needed for personal use. To exceed these limits was viewed as a threat to the entire system. Those who exceeded the limits were no longer granted the tacit support of the work group, which includes the right to neutralize one's guilt feelings and deny oneself the definition of one's acts as theft.

CONCLUSIONS

Within the limitations of this study, the following generalizations are suggested by the data. These may well serve as conditions with which a theory of blue-collar crime must be consistent:

A. *The Conception of Property Within the Work Plant:*

1   All property in the plant is cognitively mapped by the workers into three categories: personal property, corporate property, and property of uncertain ownership.

2   Each category of property consists of a continuum extending from a hard core of readily identifiable and nonmobile items to an outer fringe of uncertain, vacillatory items.

3   The hard-core items rarely shift from one category to another—the only category which is amenable to major shifts from the hard core is the category of "uncertain ownership."

4   Lacking a natural division between company property and property of uncertain ownership, *e.g.*, scrap *v.* nonscrap, usable *v.* nonusable, the work group will establish crude boundaries which will create such a division.

5   Property of uncertain ownership is comprised almost exclusively of company-owned goods and materials which are small, copious, and inexpensive. Given a work plant in which there is a strict company policy relative to pilfering, the uncertain ownership category would be almost exclusively made up of by-products which are thrown away or consumed in the production process.

B. *The Work Group Norms Governing Pilfering in the Work Plant:*

1   The work group subculture contains a set of norms which deal with pilfering in the plant. These norms, though necessarily vague, serve to provide the workers with a set of general guidelines relative to the acceptable *modus operandi,* the tolerable limits, the conditions of pilfering, etc.

2   Property of uncertain ownership is considered by the work

group as the only type of property that legitimately may be taken from the plant. Company and personal property, though sometimes taken, are done so without the sanction of the work group.

3 The pilfering of property of uncertain ownership is regarded as falling within the conventional morality, whereas the pilfering of other types of property is regarded as a violation of work group, work plant, and societal norms.

4 The work group norms cognitively map the taking of property of uncertain ownership in such a way as to take it out of the realm of theft. Theft has a victim; property of uncertain ownership lacks a victim.

5 Workers who pilfer company property or personal property, especially the latter, do so without the protection of the work group. The work group extends its protection only to those who operate within the folkways.

6 The pilferers of property of uncertain ownership are granted the protection of the work group only if they are pilfering within the tolerable limit. To exceed the limit is to risk losing the protection of the work group.

7 The work group norms do not clearly delineate what constitutes a reasonable amount of pilfering (*i.e.*, what constitutes a tolerable limit). There are, however, two broad guidelines: 1) what one needs for personal use and 2) that which will not jeopardize the system by focusing supervisory attention on the pilfering.

8 In plants where pilfering does not assume the form of a protest, team pilfering is taboo because it violates the definitions of the tolerable limit.

9 The work group norms of pilfering are assimilated through precept and work group folklore.

THE VIOLATORS' VOCABULARIES
OF ADJUSTMENT *

DONALD R. CRESSEY

After a trusted person has defined a problem as non-shareable, the total pertinent situation consists of a problem which must be solved by an independent, secret, and relatively safe means by virtue of general and technical information about trust violation. In this situation the potential trust violator identifies the possibilities for resolving the problem by violating his position of trust and defines the relationship between the non-shareable problem and the illegal solution in language which enables him to look upon trust violation (*a*) as essentially non-criminal, (*b*) as justified, or (*c*) as a part of a general irresponsibility for which he is not completely accountable. The term "rationalization" has been applied to the last phase, and it is with this process that we are concerned in this chapter.

We began using the "rationalization" terminology when it was discovered that the application of certain key verbalizations

* The editors of this volume have edited and abridged Donald R. Cressey's "The Violators' Vocabularies of Adjustment," as found in his book *Other Peoples' Money* (New York: The Free Press of Glencoe, 1953).

to his conduct enables the trusted person to "adjust" his conceptions of himself as a trusted person with his conceptions of himself as a user of entrusted funds for solving a non-shareable problem, but the use of the term in this way is not in keeping with popular usage or with usage by some sociologists, psychologists, and psychiatrists. An ordinary definition of the term indicates that rationalization takes place *after* the specific behavioral item in question has occurred. One buys an automobile and then "rationalizes" that he needs it because his health is poor. The notion here is that of an *ex post facto* justification for behavior which "has really been prompted by deeply hidden motives and unconscious tendencies." [1] But the term is also used to refer to a process of finding some logical excuse for questionable behavior tendencies,[2] for thoughts as well as acts,[3] and for decisions to perform an act.[4]

In addition, a rationalization has been considered as a verbalization which purports to make the person's behavior more intelligible to others in terms of symbols currently employed by his group.[5] It follows from this kind of definition that the person may prepare his rationalization before he acts, or he may act first and rationalize afterward. In the cases of trust violation encountered, significant rationalizations were always present *before* the criminal act took place, or at least at the time it took place, and, in fact, after the act had taken place the rationalization often was abandoned. If this observation were generalized to other behavior we would not say that an individual "buys an automobile and then rationalizes," as in the example above, but that he buys the car because he is able to rationalize. The rationalization is

[1] A. P. Noyes, *Modern Clinical Psychiatry* (Philadelphia: W. B. Saunders, 1940), p. 49. *Cf.* R. S. Woodworth, *Psychology* (New York: Henry Holt & Co., 1940), p. 537: "The question is what reason to assign for an act"; and F. L. Ruch, *Psychology and Life* (New York: Scott, Foresman & Co., 1941), p. 181: "The ascribing of false motives to one's behavior."
[2] T. W. Richards, *Modern Clinical Psychology* (New York: McGraw-Hill, 1946), p. 84.
[3] K. Young, *Personality and Problems of Adjustment* (New York: F. S. Crofts & Co., 1946), p. 122.
[4] R. T. LaPiere and P. R. Farnsworth, *Social Psychology* (New York: McGraw-Hill, 1949), p. 13.
[5] A. R. Lindesmith and A. L. Strauss, *Social Psychology* (New York: Dryden Press, 1949), p. 308.

his motivation,[6] and it not only makes his behavior intelligible to others, but it makes it intelligible to *himself.*[7]

On the present level of explanation, systematic causation, it is sufficient to indicate the presence or absence of a rationalization which, together with the knowledge that the position of trust can be violated, enables the person to perceive that the desired results may be produced by violation of the position of trust. The trusted person either uses such a rationalization or he does not. The essential point is that the person must perceive his position of trust as offering an opportunity for such violation, and that such perception, which involves the use of a rationalization, is a part of a process which begins with the structuring of a problem as non-shareable and ends with the criminal violation of financial trust. However, as indicated previously, a discussion of rationalizations used in trust violation is not entirely separable from discussion of the sources of those rationalizations.

In our hypothesis we have observed that one phase of the process which results in trust violation is the application, to the trusted person's own conduct, of language categories which enable him to adjust two rather conflicting sets of values and behavior patterns. But such verbalizations necessarily are impressed upon the person by other persons who have had prior experience with situations involving positions of trust and trust violation. Before they are internalized by the individual they exist as group definitions of situations in which crime is "appropriate." Contacts with such definitions obviously are necessary prior to their internalization as rationalizations. The following propositions, for example, are ideal-type definitions of situations in which trust violation is called for and which, hence, amount to ideologies which sanction the crime: "Some of our most respectable citizens got

---

[6] *Cf.* C. Wright Mills, "Situated Actions and Vocabularies of Motive," *American Sociological Review,* 5 (December, 1940), pp. 904–913.
[7] See Kingsley Davis, *Human Society* (New York: Macmillan, 1949), pp. 267–268. In his discussion of the specific things which are learned in association with criminal and anti-criminal behavior patterns, Sutherland apparently uses the term rationalization in this same sense, to refer to an evaluation of criminal behavior. That is, a rationalization is considered as equivalent to an attitude about the "oughtness" of the behavior as conceived by the person. E. H. Sutherland, *Principles of Criminology* (New York: Lippincott, 1947), p. 6.

their start in life by using other people's money temporarily."⁸ "In the real estate business there is nothing wrong about using deposits before the deal is closed"; "All people steal when they get in a tight spot."

The following propositions are the personalized versions of those definitions after they have been assimilated and internalized by an individual: "My intent is only to use this money temporarily so I am 'borrowing,' not 'stealing'"; "My immediate use of real estate deposits is 'ordinary business'"; "I have been trying to live an honest life but I have had nothing but troubles so 'to hell with it.'" The individual in a specific, present, situation uses such rationalizations in the adjustment of personal conflicting values, but the use of the verbalization in this way is necessarily preceded by observation of rather general criminal ideologies.

We see then that, having general information about trust violation and about the conditions under which trust violation occurs, the trust violator, upon the appearance of the non-shareable problem, applies to his own situation a rationalization which the groups in which he has had membership have applied to the behavior of others, and which he himself has applied to the behavior of others. He perceives that the general rule applies to his specific case. Such an application to himself of the symbols held by the members of his groups has been described by Mead as taking the rôle of the "generalized other."⁹ Thus, the imagination of how he appears to others, and of how he would appear if his non-shareable problem were revealed to others is a controlling "force" in the behavior of the trusted person.

In a "non-shareable-problem—position-of-trust" situation trusted persons "objectify" their own actions to the extent that they place themselves in the place of another person or group of persons with the status of "trustee" and hypothesize their reactions. The hypothesized reactions to "borrowing" in order to solve a non-shareable problem, for example, are much different from hypothesized reactions to "stealing," and the trusted person

⁸ *Cf.* Alexander Dumas, *The Money Question,* an English translation of which appears in *Poet Lore,* 26 (March–April, 1915), pp. 129–227, especially Act II: "What is business? That's easy. It's other people's money, of course."
⁹ George H. Mead, "A Behavioristic Account of the Significant Symbol," *Journal of Philosophy,* 19 (March, 1922), pp. 157–163. See also his *Mind, Self and Society* (Chicago: University of Chicago Press, 1934), pp. 135–226.

behaves accordingly. Similarly, the hypothesized reactions to a conception of self as an "ill" person or as a "pressed" person have different implications for behavior than hypothesized reactions to a conception of self as a "criminal." [10]

It is because of hypothesized reactions which do not consistently and severely condemn his criminal behavior that the trusted person takes the role of what *we* have called the "trust violator." [11] *He* often does not think of himself as playing that rôle, but often thinks of himself as playing a rôle such as that of a special kind of "borrower," "businessman," or even "thief." In order to do so,

[10] Although it was not in any way checked by her research, Redden offers the following hypothesis, based on Mead's distinction between the "I" and the "me," about the rôle-taking behavior of embezzlers. "In his rehearsal of consequences in the process of taking the rôle of another he [the embezzler] fails to integrate himself with the organized pattern of approved social behavior. He fails or refuses to try to devise a plan by reflective thinking which will increase his value to the organization and call forth recognition in terms of increased income. Thwarted in his attempt or impatient of the duration of time necessary to fulfill his wish on the socially desirable level, his mental activity is centered on a plan of borrowing, converting his employer's goods or money to his own use, to fulfill the wish for a margin above the equilibrium of income and cost of living to satisfy some latent desire in a minimum of time. He completes the act hypothetically, taking the rôle of another but contrary to the common organized pattern of social behavior in business relationships and in the social group. His hypothetical solution may be a new technique or method which if discovered by the employer would mean dismissal from his employ and community disapproval. His mental activity is in opposition to the organized sets of attitudes of the social group. The two aspects of the self of the embezzler are in conflict, the social or impersonal self integrates the hypothetical act with the organized social behavior of the group by naming the act resulting from the proposed plan borrowing, with intent to replace or repay; the other aspect of self, the personal or asocial, views his plan as opposed to organized social behavior, independent of the group and unknown to the group." Elizabeth Redden, *Embezzlement, A Study of One Kind of Criminal Behavior, With Prediction Tables Based on Fidelity Insurance Records,* Ph.D. Dissertation, University of Chicago, 1939, pp. 27–29.

[11] In this connection, we shall see later that when the long-term violator who has convinced himself that he is a "borrower" decides that he is "in too deep" the attitudes of his group toward "embezzlement" and "crime" can no longer be avoided, and his behavior takes on the characteristics of the rôle which he *then* conceives of himself as playing. Similarly, we shall see that while there exists in most groups in our culture a rather general condemnation of "trust violation" or "stealing" this condemnation is not as general when the "mitigating circumstances" are known. That is, some categories of criminal behavior are not as severely or consistently condemned as others. The trust violator behaves according to the cultural definitions of those categories.

he necessarily must have come into contact with a culture which defined those rôles for him. If the rôles were defined differently in his culture, or if he had not come into contact with the group definitions, he would behave differently.

The rationalizations used by trust violators, then, reflect contacts with cultural ideologies which themselves are contradictory to the theme that honesty is expected in all situations of trust.[12] When used by the individual, such ideologies adjust contradictory personal values in regard to criminality on the one hand and integrity, honesty and morality on the other.[13] Law-enforcement officials and judges do not officially recognize such cultural contradictions, and in individual cases they hold that trust violation perpetrated according to a rationalization derived from such an ideology is not for that reason "excusable." Trusted persons with non-shareable problems utilize rationalizations in order to select means, which otherwise would not be available to them, for solving those problems.[14] While the selection of means is recognized

[12] "When rationalizations are extensively developed and systematized as group doctrines and beliefs, they are known as ideologies. As such, they acquire unusual prestige and authority. The person who uses them has the sense of conforming to group expectations, of doing the 'right thing.' . . . Unscrupulous and sometimes criminal behavior in business and industry is justified in terms of an argument which begins and ends with the assertion that 'business is business.' . . . The principal advantage of group rationalizations or ideologies, from the individual's standpoint, is that they give him a sense of support and sanction. They help him to view himself and his activities in a favorable light and to maintain his self-esteem and self-respect." A. R. Lindesmith and A. L. Strauss, *op. cit.*, pp. 309–310. Reproduced by permission of the publisher.

[13] In a letter to the author even an official of a bonding company differentiated between "embezzlers" and "crooks" by saying: "Actually the average embezzler is no more crook than you or I. As a result of circumstances, he finds himself in some position where, with no criminal intent, he 'borrows' from his employer. One circumstance leads to another and it is only a matter of time before he is discovered and discharged with or without prosecution."

[14] The fact that trust violators use rationalizations does not mean, of course, that they are more "rational" than other persons, or that they carefully weigh and consider the advantages and disadvantages of trust violation in an objective, careful, precise manner. The use of the rationalization makes this unnecessary, and once the trusted person has rationalized the violation of his trust it is impossible for him to be concerned with the question of whether the rationalization is a "good" one.

Probably it was the observation of this sort of thing which led Lottier to the formulation of that part of his theory which holds that in cases of embezzlement there is "no subjectively available alternative" to embezzlement. S. Lottier, "Tension Theory of Criminal Behavior," *American Sociological Review*, 7 (December, 1942), pp. 840–848. Our analysis also can

by the criminal law, most of the conditions under which such rationalizations are used do not constitute "necessity" according to the legal definitions, and hence they are not considered as sufficient for avoidance of legal liability.[15] The circumstances under which the selections are made are sufficient, however, to explain theoretically why an individual criminally violates his trust rather than behaving in some other manner, even if those circumstances do not "excuse" him from legal liability.

The preceding discussion of the nature of the rationalizations used in trust violation can be elaborated and verified by further consideration of case material. The subjects can be divided into three categories, according to the system of trust violation which was used, and, significantly, to some extent in accordance with the specific nature of the rationalizations which were applied to their own conduct. The first group consists of persons who were in business for themselves and who converted "deposits" which were entrusted to them for a specific purpose while at the same time maintaining their regular business. The second group is made up of individuals who as employed persons converted their employer's funds, or funds belonging to their employer's clients, by taking relatively small amounts over a period of time. The final group overlaps the second in that it is made up of persons who converted funds or property at hand and absconded with it, whether or not they were employed by the trustor.

INDEPENDENT BUSINESSMEN

Independent businessmen who converted "deposits" which had

---

be considered as a detailed consideration of Riemer's general statement that the opportunities presented through occupancy of a position of trust form a "temptation" if the embezzler develops an "anti-social attitude" which makes possible the abandonment of the folkways of legitimate business behavior. Svend Riemer, "Embezzlement: Pathological Basis," *Journal of Criminal Law and Criminology*, 32 (November–December, 1941), pp. 411–423. As shall be shown later, however, most of the trust violators encountered did not so much abandon the folkways of legitimate business behavior as they did re-structure the situation in such a way that, from their point of view, they were *not* abandoning such folkways. Similarly, except for absconders, the attitudes of the men interviewed were not so much "anti-social" as they were "pro-social" in that the endeavor was to keep from considering themselves as criminals.

[15] Jerome Hall, *Principles of Criminal Law* (Indianapolis: Bobbs-Merrill, 1947), pp. 415–426.

been entrusted to them because of their business positions converted such deposits upon becoming aware that the entrusted funds could be used in the solution of their non-shareable problems[16] and convincing themselves either (*a*) that they were merely borrowing the money which they converted, or (*b*) that the funds entrusted to them were really theirs. Supplementing these rationalizations was the attitude that "everyone" in business in some way or other converts or misapplies deposits so that it is not entirely wrong. At least it is not as wrong as "stealing" or "robbing." The latter philosophy is not always present, but when it is, it contributes to the ease with which trusted persons use the significant rationalizations. That is, one more easily convinces himself that he is "borrowing" rather than "stealing" if he feels that other persons in his particular type of business have "borrowed" money in the same way and repaid it. One violator (Case 120) told of a man who had behaved just as the violator did but who had made a considerable amount of money rather than being sent to prison. The informant's position was that this person had received "breaks" which he himself did not get, and that that was the only real difference between the two persons. Other violators related similar accounts.

BORROWING   In most instances the rationalization that the conversion of deposits would merely amount to "borrowing" the deposits for a short time was an easy and logical step to make, since the ordinary practice of the businessmen interviewed was similar to such borrowing. Most of the real estate dealers and automobile salesmen spontaneously pointed this out. One former real estate dealer, for example, expressed the position by asking for the interviewer's response to the question (Case 97): "If you had $10

[16] The non-shareable problems possessed by the members of this group ordinarily were related to business reversals or to considerations of having made "foolish" investments, but this was not true in two cases. Also, the violation of trust by members of this group may be characterized generally by Riemer's phrase, "embezzlement of the entrepreneur in his struggle for economic independence." He describes such entrepreneurs as follows: "During . . . economic depression these new entrepreneurs meet a previously unexperienced situation. . . . Speculation and scheming has been the basis of their previous success. They cling to this attitude for self-defense, finally overstepping the borderline of legal business transactions. . . . It is the sudden reverse in the trend of the economic career and lack of previous experiences to meet the emergency situation which predominate in the causation of the crime." Svend Riemer, *op. cit.*

in the bank but no money with you right now and I gave you $5 so that you could get some cigarettes for me in the morning, what would you do with that $5 if the man across the hall wanted to sell you his $15 pen for $5 when you leave this room?" The implication was that the $5 would be used and that the money for the cigarettes would be drawn out of the bank in the morning. The informant went on to explain that he and other businessmen had always conducted their business along those lines, but that finally the situation in his case was such that, in terms of the example, he did not have the $10 to "cover" the $5 he "borrowed."

OWNERSHIP Like the idea of "borrowing," the rationalization that converted funds really "belong to" the trusted person also frequently comes from the extension of a customary business practice which, although often considered by violators to be unethical, is not ordinarily considered as criminal. We refer to the practice of spending the profits of a business negotiation before the deal is actually consummated. Trust violators claim that it is usual business practice to accept deposits on goods and then, before the goods actually are delivered, to use part of the money deposited, on the assumption that before the delivery date enough money for the purchase of the goods will be secured elsewhere. In solving a non-shareable problem they similarly used the deposited money for themselves, on the assumption that it need not be accounted for—*i.e.*, that it "belonged to" them. Just as in many cases of "borrowing," the independent businessmen who used this rationalization often were at first able to "cover" the situation if an unforeseen event made it necessary to return the money or consummate the deal at a time earlier than was expected, and in that event, of course, the reasoning that the funds belonged to them was reinforced. And when the person's own source of income or means of security was cut off in such a way that he could not "cover" the converted funds he simply continued to rationalize that the entrusted funds were really his, just as they were when he was able to cover them.

THE UNUSUAL SITUATION All of the trust violators who were interviewed were asked to tell not only what they thought was the cause of their own behavior but also what they thought was the general cause or causes of the type of crime of which they were convicted.[17] Because of the nature of the non-shareable problems and the rationalizations which preceded the crimes of the members of the group under consideration, the usual response to the first question was an explanation in terms of an extraordinary situation. One of the violators causally remarked, typically, that there was nothing unusual about him but that the *situation* was unusual, and then he went on to say that the average businessman just doesn't run into that kind of situation. According to our theory, the reason the "situations" are unusual, or seem to be to the independent businessmen, lies in the fact that they contain non-shareable financial problems which, in almost all cases, have resulted from prior business activities.

In response to the second question, most of the businessmen expressed the opinion that in the usual, average, or typical case the person gets into difficulty with the law because he is a gambler, lives on a high level, or associates with "other women." They then added that in their own cases this did not take place—they did not gamble, live beyond their means, etc.—and then they repeated the view that they were merely unfortunate businessmen who had run into an unusual situation. Because they believed that trust violators are persons who get into trouble with the law because of some kind of "immoral" behavior, while at the same time they considered their own conduct to have been related to an unusual business trend, these men did not ordinarily consider themselves to be criminals.[18]

LONG-TERM VIOLATORS

Those trust violators whose peculations had extended over a period of time were of special value in development of the gener-

[17] The latter question was asked because it was anticipated that the subjects would "project" their own experiences into the general explanation, giving additional information about their own cases. This occurred in a few instances, but the ordinary response indicated that rather than projecting his own case into the general explanation the individual was *excepting* his own conduct from the general explanation or explanations with which he was familiar. This practice is theoretically significant, and is discussed in the final chapter. Donald R. Cressey, *op. cit.*

[18] In addition to excusing themselves on the ground that there had been no prior "immoral" behavior in their cases, independent businessmen also insisted that there was no crime because the intent was to repay the money, because the misappropriation was unintentional, because an offer of restitution was made, or because the transaction was "ordinary business."

alization since in their cases it was possible to observe not only the consequences to trust violation of the application of the rationalization to their own conduct, but the consequences of abandonment of the rationalization at a later time as well. Violators of this class usually, like the independent businessmen, convert entrusted funds only after rationalizing that they are merely borrowing the money. Other rationalizations were observed, but they ordinarily existed in conjunction with the foregoing conception of the use of the funds. For example some of the violators of this kind rationalized that they were embezzling only to keep their families from shame, disgrace, or poverty, that theirs was a case of "necessity," that their employers were cheating them and were dishonest, so that trust violation seemed justified. But in almost all instances these rationalizations were subsidiary to the rationalization that the money was merely being borrowed from the employer or his clients in order to meet the demands of a nonshareable problem.

In fact, we interviewed only five employed persons who took money over a period of time who did not use the specific verbalization that they were merely borrowing the money. In the first of these cases a man who said that his employer had failed to keep his promises in regard to the conditions of employment[19] and salary admitted setting out deliberately to embezzle funds in order to get the promised salary. He had a history of other frauds, and claimed to have been associated with famous confidence men of a past generation. In spite of this, he apparently accepted the position of trust in good faith, told his employer about his past criminal record, and got along all right until the management changed hands, due to the death of his sponsor.

In another case (Case 51) the violator also was an ex-convict, although his incarceration had been for a crime of a different nature and he had held trusted positions for eight years between his release from prison and his present position. He was apprehended in an attempt to secure his employer's funds by the simple expedient of opening a new bank account in his employer's name

---

[19] A pamphlet advertising the services of a bonding company has the following to say about the working conditions of employees: "Good environment is conducive to the honest performance of duty. Employees who are underpaid, overworked or abused, often steal from their employers without compunction. *They feel that they have it coming.*" Continental Casualty Company, *Crime Loss Prevention* (Chicago: Author, 1947), p. 14.

and depositing funds in it. He expressed an exceptionally intense antagonistic attitude toward his employer. His rationalization was similar to that in Case 52, as were the rationalizations of the persons in the other three cases (12, 61, 94), all of whose non-shareable problems also resulted from the relationship with the employer.[20]

BORROWING   All of the long-term violators interviewed indicated that some problem had been structured as non-shareable, and the large proportion using the rationalization that they were merely borrowing the money which was converted is indicative of the significance which this verbalization has for trust violation of this kind. This rationalization is used initially by trusted employees in much the same manner that it is used by independent business-men.

IMPLICATIONS FOR OVERT BEHAVIOR   The trusted employees under consideration here at first looked upon themselves not as criminals but as borrowers,[21] and they behaved accordingly, so that the

[20] Wesley Price, "How to Rob a Bank," *Saturday Evening Post*, 219 (March 2, 1946) pp. 12–13*ff*., cites the somewhat comparable case of a bank employee who decided that his salary was $1500 less per year than he was worth, and who embezzled exactly $1500 a year until his salary finally was raised to the amount which he thought he deserved. Later, when his salary was raised to a figure above that amount, he repaid the excess each month, still under the impression that he was worth the amount stipulated. In this case it is quite apparent that the employee did *not* have the aim of per-manently depriving his employer of the money, but only to "borrow" what he considered his "just" income until such time as his salary was raised. Hence, the rationalization that he was not stealing but that he was merely "bor-rowing" the amount necessary was a crucial element in all of his peculations. Because he carefully controlled the amount taken he never did look upon his behavior as criminal. The five subjects we have cited from our own cases did look upon their behavior as criminal, but they considered it to be justified under the circumstances as they construed them.

[21] The recognition that he rationalized, often, in fact, works a hardship on the prisoner since he does not ordinarily comprehend that he behaved in terms of the rationalization available at the time of the defalcation, not at the time of imprisonment. Those who wonder how they possibly could have considered that they were "merely borrowing" or that their behavior was not dishonest become disturbed when they cannot provide an answer. For instance, the subject who seemed to be doing the "hardest time" in prison was one who insisted that he had been "merely rationalizing" that he was going to repay the funds when he was embezzling, while at the same time he was unable to provide himself with an acceptable alternative explanation for his embezzlement. One by one he eliminated all of the explanations which he considered, becoming more and more uncomfortable because of

manner in which the trust was violated consisted of taking relatively small amounts of money over a period of time. They did not at first consider the possibility of absconding with the funds just as they did not consider the possibility of committing another type of crime. In the conception of one's rôle as that of a "borrower" such considerations are unnecessary.

In a few instances, such as in Case 220, trust violators of this sort kept a careful record of the amount of their "indebtedness" but in most instances in which the peculations have extended over a period of time the employed person becomes genuinely in doubt about the amount of money taken. This is due to the fact that after a few transactions of which no record is kept, violators usually are no longer concerned about each manipulation. Trust violation becomes somewhat routine to them and they come to look upon the source of their illegally obtained funds as a rather general "pool" or "pot" from which they can readily abstract funds at will.[22] Looking at the source of income in this way and continuing to rationalize that the funds are only being borrowed, a considerable amount of money is taken before trust violators realize that they cannot possibly repay the amount taken. This realization, which is described as recognition of the fact that they are "in too deep" [23] does not occur in all cases, since some viola-

---

his inability to account for his behavior. Finally he concluded that there must have been an emotional or psychiatric disorder present. He planned to visit a psychiatrist upon release. In this case, and in others like it, the subject had, before apprehension, recognized independently that he was "in too deep" and could not possibly repay the amount of money he had taken. As was the case with independent businessmen, those who were apprehended before they came to this conclusion did not look upon themselves as criminals, even after they had been convicted.

[22] In a personal interview, an officer of a surety bonding company had the following to say about the use of the "borrowing" verbalization:

"In the banking business they get a young fellow as teller and pay him $100 or $125 a month, and you know how much you can do with that, and they put him right in the middle of temptation. He finds it hard going and first thing you know he gets an idea into his head that here's a way to get some ready cash. Not that he intends to steal it. Oh, no! That's furthest from his intention. It's just a loan. They all take it with the intention of paying back, but somehow they get in deeper and deeper until they are caught."

[23] Although legally the violator who rationalizes that he is borrowing is classified as a trust violator from the beginning, it is when he feels that

tors are arrested before it takes place, and its absence enables
the trust violators to continue rationalizing, even after apprehension, that they were merely borrowing the money.

Those who realize that they are "in too deep" are forced
to recognize that their reasoning in regard to borrowing has
been "phony" or that they have been "kidding themselves" about
repaying the money. This conclusion is not drawn when the total
peculations reach some specific amount or after the trust violation
has extended over a particular period of time. Instead, various
violators reported that it occurred to them that they were "in too
deep" when they added up the total amount taken, read an article
in a newspaper about an embezzlement case, observed another
embezzlement case in their own company, observed that it was
physically impossible to return the money without detection, or
in some other way became concerned with the facts of the defalcation. One violator claimed that he was in bed when it suddenly
occurred to him that he had not been borrowing but embezzling
instead, and he described the process as being similar to awaken-
ing from a dream. When they realize that they have not been borrowing, the violators define themselves as criminals, find this
definition incompatible with their positions as trusted persons,
and usually condemn themselves for their past behavior.

However, all of the long-term violators (and also the independent businessmen) who used the rationalization that they
were borrowing, pointed out that even before there was a consideration of being "in too deep" or a good chance of detection
there was a desire to "clear the whole thing up" as soon as possible. This desire to repay at this point is indicative of an attempt
to continue membership in a social order which condemns embezzlement, theft, crime, etc., but which does not so stringently
condemn borrowing, even of the sort which is done surrepti-
tiously by a bank teller. By conceiving of himself as a borrower
the violator cuts himself off from the influences of a social order
which otherwise would deter him, and before he gets in too deep
he is not fully cognizant of the social attitudes which later induce

---

he is "in too deep" that he identifies with criminals, if he ever does. His
belief that he is in too deep comes at a point where he recognizes that he
is unable to repay what he has borrowed, but, as we can see in this case,
this is also the point at which he considers that his employer, bonder, or
community would consider his offense as more than a mere "technical violation" in the event that it were discovered.

him to behave like a criminal. While he is able to look upon his behavior as borrowing, his desire is to repay the money borrowed and not, as may be the case later, to avoid being caught and sent to prison. At the beginning the fear, if there is any, is a fear of losing his social position through exposure of the non-shareable problem, not the fear of punishment or imprisonment. The trust violator cannot fear the treatment usually accorded criminals until he comes to look upon himself as a criminal.

Hence, by using the rationalization that they are borrowing, trust violators are able to remain in full contact with the values and ideals of former and present associates who condemn crime, and when they find that they are "in too deep" and have slipped into a category (criminal) which they know is regarded as undesirable according to that set of values and ideals, they rebel against it. They usually describe themselves as being extremely nervous, tense, emotionally upset, and unhappy, and to get rid of these symptoms they behave in rather incongruous fashion.[24] On the one hand, they may report their behavior to the police or to their employer, quit taking funds or resolve to quit taking funds, speculate or gamble wildly in order to regain the amounts taken, or "leave the field" by absconding or committing suicide. This behavior also is indicative of an attempt to maintain membership in a social order which condemns crime and considers honesty as an ideal. On the other hand, they may become reckless in their defalcations, taking larger amounts than formerly with less attempt to avoid detection and with no notion of repayment.[25] This behavior is indicative of at least partial acceptance of the values of the new group (criminals) with whom they are now identified.

In the absence of the rationalization that he is borrowing, then, a trust violator of this kind cannot reconcile the fact that he is converting money while at the same time he is an honest and trusted person. As a result, he either (*a*) readopts the attitudes of the groups with which he identified before he violated his trust,

[24] The behavior here may be described as an inability to adjust to the new rôle. For a general discussion of problems of adjustment to social rôles, see L. S. Cottrell, "The Adjustment of the Individual to his Age and Sex Rôles," *American Sociological Review,* 7 (October, 1942), pp. 617–620.
[25] Upon apprehension, persons who behave in either of these ways may attempt to "fix" their cases. This practice varies from seeing the trustor or bonding company and offering restitution, to having a friend invite a judge or prosecuting attorney to dinner.

or (*b*) he adopts the attitudes of the new category of persons (criminals) with whom he now identifies himself.

All the violators who had "exceeded their limits" and had come to look upon their behavior as criminal seemed to sincerely regret the initial peculation, saying that if it had not occurred, the non-shareable problem would have cleared itself up somehow, and at any rate, they would not be in such a bad condition as they were in prison. A few of them reported that instead of aiding in the solution of their problem as they had anticipated, trust violation had only resulted in the substitution of one non-shareable problem for another. The original desire was to solve the non-shareable problem, but when the violators finally admitted to themselves that they were not able to repay, and that their behavior was criminal, the desire often was to avoid exposure of the crime also. In the absence of the rationalization that the money was being borrowed, the positions of trust were no longer perceived as providing solutions for either non-shareable problem and, in fact, those problems were exposed.

In summary, trust violators who take funds over a period of time by rationalizing that they are borrowing the money become criminals without intending to do so.[26] The position of trust is perceived as providing a solution to a non-shareable problem when, in the trust violator's words, the individual "kids himself" or uses "phony reasoning" that he is going to repay the amounts taken. Without this rationalization the series of peculations would not have begun. In prison those trust violators who finally come to

[26] Some of those interviewed actually used the words "accidental violation" to refer to their behavior. We do not intend to imply that meaning in any of our statements. The Continental Casualty Company describes the embezzlement process in which the "borrowing" rationalization is used as a "vicious cycle": "The average dishonest employee is an anomaly in the field of crime. Usually he has advanced to a position of trust by above average ability, ambition to progress and willingness to accept responsibility, coupled with faithful application to duty throughout a long period of employment. His background, both business and personal, is above reproach and without indication of instability to act as a warning against possible dishonesty. Yet, due to some 'emergency' need for money, this employee succumbs to temptation. The first misstep is usually a relatively small matter, a 'temporary loan' which he expects to pay when he receives his next pay check, but having stolen once it becomes easier to do so again and in time he is unable to extricate himself from the vicious cycle he has set in motion. Eventually the theft is discovered and rarely is it possible to effect restitution." Continental Casualty Company, *op. cit.*, p. 5. Reproduced by permission of the publisher.

look upon their behavior as criminal express general disapproval of crime and trust violation, just as do non-prisoners. While incarcerated, they are able to state that they were just "kidding themselves" that they were going to repay the money, and they point out that after they "got in too deep" they were forced to abandon this kind of "kidding" and face the serious fact that they were behaving in a criminal manner. If the amount of the peculations does not get to the point where the individual feels that he can no longer handle it, he never does look upon himself as a genuine criminal, even if he has been incarcerated for his behavior.

ABSCONDERS [27]

While among persons who abscond with entrusted funds, as among other violators, almost any problem situation may be defined as non-shareable, the problems which are non-shareable for absconders are almost always of that nature, at least in part because the person is physically isolated from other persons with whom he can share his problems. Individuals who abscond with the funds or goods entrusted to them usually are unmarried or separated from their spouses, live in hotels or rooming houses, have few primary group associations of any sort, and own little property. Only one of the absconders interviewed had held a higher status position of trust, such as accountant, business executive, or bookkeeper. The others had been employed as oil station attendants, salesmen, hotel clerks, truck drivers, bill collectors, and the like. While we cannot generalize that the members of this group are always persons with few primary group contacts and persons of lower socio-economic status, it does appear that the rationalizations which are used by absconders are more readily available to persons with such characteristics than they are to other trusted persons.

Individuals who violate positions of trust by absconding deliberate for varying periods of time on the question of whether or not they should abscond and then conclude that their attempts

[27] By absconders we mean those persons who violate their trust by removing funds or goods entrusted to them and then severing connections with the trustor by leaving his employment or leaving the vicinity. We do not include men who, for example, take relatively small amounts of money over a period of time, then disappear when they think they are "in too deep."

to conduct their lives on an honest basis have been futile, that they don't care what happens to them, that they can't help themselves because the criminality "in" people comes out in circumstances such as those in which they find themselves. This rationalization was used by all persons who absconded with the money or property at hand. By rationalizing that they no longer "care" what happens to them and that crime is "in" them, they are able to look upon themselves as almost completely lacking in accountability for their criminal acts.

The lack of primary group relationships and the lower occupational status of trust violators of this kind not only make rather ordinary problems non-shareable, but they contribute to the ease with which the rationalization is used since the situation is such that the person can abscond by severing a minimum of social ties. Primary group members both define goals for the individual and "control" him by invoking prescribed rules for the attainment of those goals. In the absence of such groups the individual is not clearly cognizant of "appropriate" goals nor of "appropriate" means for attaining them.[28] For the person who has a minimum of obligations of a legitimate nature, such as support of a family or maintenance of property interests,[29] it is relatively easy to rationalize that he "doesn't care" if the criminality which is "in" him comes out and, consequently, to disappear with the funds.

In one sense, absconders "escape" from the conflict situation present when they have a non-shareable problem and no apparent honest way of solving it. Rather than structuring the situation in such a way that trust violation does not at first seem dishonest, as is the case in almost all instances of violation by employees of higher social status, absconders solve their problems by structuring the situation so that the values they have formerly held have no meaning for them. Although they recognize their

[28] *Cf.* Robert K. Merton, "Social Structure and Anomie," *American Sociological Review*, 3 (October, 1938), pp. 672–682, and P. H. Landis, *Social Control* (New York: Lippincott, 1939), pp. 151–166. Both of these authors point out that definite pressure upon certain persons to engage in nonconformist conduct is exerted in social structures in which either the goals, the means of attaining them, or the relationship between the goals and the means are loosely defined for the individual.

[29] The effect of such obligations as a deterrent to running away is recognized informally by prison officials who more readily grant "trustee" status to prisoners who have property or families in the state where the prison is located than to prisoners who do not have such obligations.

behavior as criminal from the beginning, they rationalize in such a way that they conceive of themselves as not entirely responsible for that behavior. They can't control what is "in" them. Later, usually after they have been apprehended and are completely removed from the situation, they again become cognizant of these values and decide that prior to absconding they were only "kidding" themselves into thinking that the renounced values had no meaning. They wonder how they could have done that, cannot provide an adequate answer, and this reaffirms the original belief that crime is "in" them.

THE "DON'T-CARE" ATTITUDE The verbalizations used in the absconders' conversations with themselves prior to the violation of trust accurately indicate the origin of this condition of irresponsibility or recklessness and its significance in the violation. The absconders usually describe themselves as having had a "to hell with it" attitude, although the phrases used were sometimes either more or less colorful than that. About 80 per cent of the Illinois absconders described their behavior in these terms even before the interviewer recognized that there was uniformity in this respect.

UNUSUAL PERSONAL MAKEUP Unlike the independent businessmen who, as prisoners, explained that their violation was due to an unusual *situation,* the members of this group said that their crimes were due to *personal* defects. After apprehension, absconders did not consider the situation in which they had found themselves prior to absconding to have been extraordinary, and when they remembered how they had behaved in that situation, the belief that their crime was due to a personal defect was reinforced. In both instances the criminal's explanation is related to the conception of himself which he had at the time of his violation. After apprehension these conceptions of the person's relationship in the situation were transformed into "explanations" of the crime. The independent businessmen went on thinking of themselves as ordinary businessmen who had found it necessary to cut some corners in order to meet an unusual situation, while the absconders went on thinking of themselves as having criminality in them. The businessman who has been apprehended for violation of trust considers that he lost control of a situation, while the absconder considers that he lost control of himself.

SUMMARY AND CONCLUSIONS

1   The rationalizations which are used by trust violators are necessary and essential to criminal violation of trust. They are not merely *ex post facto* justifications for conduct which already has been enacted, but are pertinent and real "reasons" which the person has for acting. When the relationship between a personal non-shareable problem and the position of trust is perceived according to the bias induced by the presence of a rationalization which makes trust violation in some way justified, trust violation results.

2   Each trusted person does not invent a new rationalization for his violation of trust, but instead he applies to his own situation a verbalization which has been made available to him by virtue of his having come into contact with a culture in which such verbalizations are present. Cultural ideologies which sanction trust violation are in basic contradiction to ideologies which hold non-violation as the norm, and in trust violation the trusted person applies a general rule to his specific case.

3   The rationalizations used in trust violation are linked with the manner in which the trust is violated and to some extent with the social and economic position of the offender. A large majority of the independent businessmen and trusted employees who take funds over a period of time apply to a situation in which a non-shareable problem is present the rationalization that they are merely borrowing the funds. The application of this rationalization has obvious implications for the behavior of the person using it, since he considers that he is playing the rôle of the borrower rather than of the trust violator. When other rationalizations are used, the person behaves accordingly. Frequently it is necessary for an individual to abandon the rationalizations which he has been using, and when this occurs he looks upon himself as a criminal. Trusted persons who abscond with the funds or property entrusted to them have previously perceived the relationship between the position of trust and a non-shareable problem according to a rationalization which makes cultural ideals in regard to honesty and "responsibility" ineffective. This rationalization

is of such a nature that the individual looks upon his rôle in violation as that of a criminal, but he thinks of himself as a special kind of "thief" rather than as a "borrower," "embezzler," or "trust violator."

AN EMPIRICAL STUDY OF
INCOME-TAX COMPLIANCE*

HAROLD M. GROVES

INTRODUCTION[1]

Studies of tax compliance in the United States have been aggregate studies proceeding either by intensive audit of a sample of
the universe of federal income-tax returns[2] or by a comparison
of income estimates with income reported for tax purposes.[3]
These studies were pioneering ventures that provided illuminating and highly important information. But they had certain in-

* The author is Professor of Economics at the University of Wisconsin.
[1] This is the first of two articles on income-tax compliance and administration, and is to found in the *National Tax Journal*, XI: 4 (December, 1958),
pp. 241–301. The second article will be published in a subsequent issue. The
studies were financed in large part by a grant from the Rockefeller
Foundation.
[2] U.S. Treasury Department, *The Audit Control Program*, May, 1951.
[3] Selma F. Goldsmith, "Appraisal of Basic Data Available for Constructing
Income Size Distributions," *Conference on Research in Income and Wealth*
(New York: National Bureau of Economic Research, 1951), Vol. 13, pp.
267–377; Daniel M. Holland and C. Harry Kahn, "Comparison of Personal
and Taxable Income," *Federal Tax Policy for Economic Growth and Sta-
bility*, Joint Committee on the Economic Report, 84th Congress, 1st Session,
1955, pp. 313–338.

herent limitations[4] and the full detail uncovered by the audit study was never disclosed to the public. It seemed to us desirable therefore to attempt some research that would start at the other end of the stick so to speak; that is, a project that would make an intensive study of a particular area. Such a study would have the limitation that it would not afford results that could be generalized nationally; however, it might have the advantage that it would disclose the anatomy of noncompliance in greater detail than other approaches and that it might suggest a methodology that could, with suitable resources and a more general access to income-tax returns, be used by others to give definitive answers as to the degree of noncompliance and its breakdown. By coupling the study with some examination of administrative techniques (future article), we hoped to indicate ways and means by which the latter could be improved.

More specifically the proposal was to ascertain unreported income and failure to comply with tax obligations by a territorial and sector-of-income approach, hunting with a shotgun, so to speak, where an auditor hunts with a rifle. We would ascertain income by source for a small block of the income-tax universe and use every means available to do so—interviews (especially with the *payers of income*); estimates of expense backed by intensive study of the area; and many other items of supplementary information differing with each source studied. Results obtained would be checked against the returns rendered and nonreporting of income would, where possible, be translated into noncompliance with tax obligations.

A Wisconsin study was indicated both by the fact that returns are uniquely available in that state and because the Wisconsin Tax Department pledged its full cooperation. The pledge was fully honored; without this assistance the study would have been impossible. Income-tax compliance in Wisconsin should be a case of compliance at its best, because here relatively good overlapping federal and state administrations reenforce each other. Checking Wisconsin returns would not be conclusive as to federal reporting, but it would be highly indicative; cooperation between administrators has developed to the point where little difference in product is expected.

Whether any of these studies was successful in accomplish-

[4] Discussed in the subsequent article.

ing its objectives we leave to the reader. Certainly many more difficulties were encountered than had been expected. Studies of interest, dividends, rent, and farm income were attempted. Attention will be given the rent study because we regard it as the most definitive.

The study of rent here reported [5] was confined to residential rent in one Wisconsin city.[6] Our study excluded commercial rent and residential rent received by corporations. It is not unlikely that compliance scores in the case of these types of rent would prove higher than for the type studied. Excluded also were structures characterized by rental transiency—hotels and motels and other structures not amenable to our type of investigation, such as hospitals, dormitories, army barracks, fraternities, and so forth.

First task involved the selection of a sample that would give each landlord of rented residential property a designated, equal probability of being selected in a sample of landlords. We cannot attempt to describe the process in detail here and shall have to impose upon the reader's credulity to share our confidence that it was performed with ample care and advice.[7] By using a building structure as the unit of sampling, it was possible to interview all of the renters of a particular structure, or at least all the renters necessary to establish with some certainty the amount of gross rent arising from the building. In turn, this full accounting of rental payments could then be related to comparable data

[5] Most of the work on this study was done by Milton Taylor, then a member of our staff and now Professor of Economics at Michigan State University.
[6] A further study of residential rent in a Wisconsin village was attempted but for reasons that need not be explained here the results were not regarded as dependable.
[7] The procedure involved the development of a probability model. The sample unit selected was the "structure" which was used either in whole or in part for residential purposes. A two-stage sampling procedure was used with a between-block interval of 3 and a within-block interval of 6. Blocks with more than average numbers of renters and structures were so handled as to double their probability of falling in the sample. The size of the sample, we should concede, was determined more by resources of time and staff than by technical criteria of adequacy. The adequacy factor could not be tested; we are confident that the results as a whole are representative for the particular city studied; they are not adequate for all of the detailed breakdown as later indicated; and, of course, their representativeness for other cities or the country as a whole are matters we have not studied.

from the income-tax returns of the landlords. Our sample included 335 landlords[8] which was 6.2 per cent of the estimated number of residential rented structures.

Precautions were taken to do a proper job of interviewing: personnel were carefully chosen and instructed, a preliminary questionnaire was pretested, and so forth. While the purpose of the interview was not fully revealed to the parties interviewed,[9] precaution was taken at every stage to guarantee the confidential character of data pertaining to particular individuals. It was apparent from the outset that a research objective and an enforcement purpose could not be combined.

Out of an original total of 1129 structures, 625 units were found to be owner-occupied; there were 86 instances of "nonresponse" in which it was not possible (3 calls) to make contact with persons living in the selected buildings; an additional 65 cases proved to be unusable for a variety of reasons, such as a vacancy or ambiguous information. There were 26 cases in which persons living in the selected buildings refused to be interviewed. A few other cases were eliminated because of ambiguities on tax returns: the reporting of several properties in an aggregate account, reporting of only gross or net data, and the like.

Classified by type of facility our sample included 205 cases of multiple units (apartments and flats); 63 cases of rooms; 48 cases of single-unit structures; 8 of garages, and 11 of subletting. The multiple-unit cases varied in character from so-called "flats," usually with 3 or less units including the unit occupied by the owner, to large apartment houses ranging to over 100 apartments. Rooming facilities included both "incidental rooming" and "operating a rooming house."

[8] 324 structures plus 11 cases of subletting.
[9] Our research team was confronted with this dilemma: in the interest of honesty and public relations we would have much preferred to have made a clean breast of "what we were up to"; in the interest of obtaining all the information we needed, the consensus was that this might prove fatal. We resolved on the basis of what we considered the public interest in favor of an honest but limited disclosure. This leaves us open to the charge of obtaining information on false, or at any rate not fully disclosed, pretenses. And it raises questions as to how frequently such research could be repeated. One might suppose that the American people would voluntarily cooperate in providing information that might disclose tax delinquency for other people . . . but it is at least doubtful that such is the case.

It seemed advisable to make a distinction in our data according to the responses of tenants. Cases were classified depending on whether the estimate of gross rent was considered to be "good," "average," or "poor"; approximately 32 per cent, 54 per cent, and 13 per cent of the cases fell into these categories, respectively. The first two classes we considered substantially reliable and the third less dependable but not useless; clearly ambiguous and incomplete cases were deleted from the sample.

In the class of multiple units we found 182 cases and $304,-865 of estimated gross rent available for comparisons with tax returns. The comparison yielded the following results: there were 8 cases, totaling $11,261 in estimated rent, in which landlords filed an income-tax return but did not declare rental income; there were 23 cases totaling $25,686 in estimated rent where no income-tax return was filed; in the remaining 151 cases, totaling $257,917 in estimated rent, landlords filed income-tax returns and declared rental income: here a direct comparison between estimated and reported rent was possible.

The eight cases in which landlords reported no rental income when filing their income-tax returns represent the clearest instance of noncompliance. It amounts to nearly 4 per cent of total estimated gross rent. Only two of the eight cases represent sizeable amounts, one for $3,961 and the other for $3,810. The 23 cases for which no income-tax returns were filed represent a persuasive but not altogether certain case of noncompliance. Care was first taken to ensure that there was no ambiguity with regard to ownership. Both property-tax data and the records of the Register of Deeds were checked. Then in each of the 23 cases, city directories and telephone books were examined to confirm that landlords had a filing liability in the city during the relevant year. The main apparent technical chance of error is the misfiling of income-tax returns, but this happens very infrequently.[10] Seven out of the 23 cases had an estimated gross rent of less than $600 (Wisconsin's filing limit), and if these rental incomes were the only source of taxable income to the landlords, the latter would have no filing liability. Calculations were made both on the as-

[10] A test of filing accuracy was attempted. The only factor of accuracy that could be examined was that of faithfulness in following the alphabet. Six hundred twenty folders were examined, out of which 11 were misplaced. However, in almost all of these cases the out-of-place folder was within a few files of the proper place and could be found easily.

sumption that these cases involved a filing liability and that they did not. On the first assumption, that all 23 cases involved a filing liability, the noncompliance on the part of non-filers represents 8 per cent of the total estimated gross rent of this class of landlords.

The remaining 151 cases reporting rent reported generally quite faithfully; the understatement of gross rent amounted to only $8,236 or nearly 3 per cent of the total estimated gross rent from all multiple-unit cases.

The total score in the reporting of estimated gross rent for multiple-unit structures was determined within a range of 85.18 per cent to 86.18 per cent, depending on the assumptions regarding non-filers explained above. Further detail was computed to show a breakdown by flats and apartments, but concerning this we can only record here that the latter showed a considerably better score.

Space does not permit a similar analysis of other types of facilities where similar but not identical problems were encountered and were similarly treated. Table 1 presents a summary of gross-rent noncompliance by types of units and indicates a composite score of 80 per cent to 81 per cent for all types combined. It will be noted that renter subletting and garages show a very low level of compliance, but they are also relatively unimportant in the total picture and our sample in these cases is too small to be reliable. A further datum may be added, namely that of those who filed and reported rent in the overall picture the figures reported were 96 per cent of the estimates.

Landlords may evade net rental income on tax returns in two ways, either through the under-reporting of gross income or through the exaggeration of expenses. In moving from gross to net rentals in our estimates it was not possible to follow the procedure used in developing the estimates for gross rentals. Tenants were found to be very vague concerning such items of expense as repairs and maintenance. They would recall that a plumber had been on the premises, for example, but they did not know whether he changed a washer or undertook a major repair. And, of course, renters usually have no knowledge at all concerning such expense items as depreciation, interest, and utilities. Interviewing landlords in order to obtain reliable information also proved to be unsatisfactory.

Decision was made to derive significant ratios through interviewing a sample of property-management experts. The ratios of interest were the average net return that may be expected on capital invested in rental housing and the ratio of expense to gross income (or alternatively of net to gross income) that may be expected with each of several types of rented property. Interviews were consummated with 17 different real-estate firms in the selected city. There was a marked consensus of opinion among the persons interviewed. Invariably the interviewee stated, for example, that the net return on capital invested in flats was within a range of 8 to 10 per cent, while single units earned a net return of 4 or 5 per cent. The percentages we accepted were an arithmetic average of all these estimates. The consensus was that expenses run to about 50 per cent of gross regardless of the type of structure.

As an alternative, we also employed the technique of reconstructing expense items for each individual property. A number of expense items like property taxes, water expense, interest, and depreciation could be and were checked specifically for each property. Certain other items, such as repairs and maintenance and heating expense, could be approximated by "rules of thumb." Illustrative is the belief among real-estate men that repairs and maintenance require on the average one month's gross rental. Some landlords will spend more than this amount for repairs and maintenance while others will spend less. Average costs of heating were computed by engineering consultants who are familiar with the relative costs and efficiencies of various fuels and the proportionate variation in costs associated with different sizes and types of structures. Average consumption costs of gas and electricity were supplied by the local utility company. And so on. There were a few miscellaneous items, such as fire insurance and advertising, for which we found no basis for approximation, but their importance in the total picture was small and we accepted in these cases the amounts claimed on returns.

On the basis of the above approaches, three independent estimates with some exceptions were made of expenses by types of units and types of expense. In some cases the ratio methods proved unfeasible. This was particularly true in the special case of incidental renting of rooms in the room-rent category. In this area quite a few cases were found too where landlords neglected

Table 1
Summary of Gross Rent Noncompliance for All Types of Units

Type of unit	Number of cases	Estimated rent	Reported rent	Noncompliance	Ratio of nonreported gross rent to estimated	Ratio of reported gross rent to estimated
Multiple units	182	$304,865	$259,681	$42,220 to $45,184	13.84 to 14.82	85.84 to 86.16
Rooms	62	52,739	35,459	16,747 to 17,280	31.76 to 32.77	67.23 to 68.24
Single units	47	41,342	26,776	13,876 to 14,567	33.54 to 35.24	64.76 to 66.46
Renter subletting	10	4,484	1,006	2,872 to 3,478	63.95 to 77.46	22.44 to 36.05
Garages	8	495	193	302	61.01	38.99
Total	309	$403,925	$323,113	$76,008 to $80,811	18.62 to 20.01	79.99 to 81.18

to deduct all of the expenses to which they were entitled. An allowance for calculated expense was added in these cases. Where the three methods were used the estimates showed very little variation in results. Ultimate answers (ratios of reported to estimated net rent) differed in no case by more than 5 per cent. In our final calculations we averaged these results.

It may be noted at this point that any relative understatement of gross rent is magnified substantially in percentage terms when it is related to net income. Assume a hypothetical business with a gross income of $100 and a ratio of expense to gross income of 50 per cent. Assume further that all expenses are properly reported and that accordingly the true net income is $50. Assume now that gross is under-reported by 20 per cent; this gives us the following data:

Gross income....................	$100
Reported gross.................	80
Expenses......................	50
Reported net...................	30
True net......................	50
Ratio of reported to true net income	60

If now we also assume that expenses are over-reported to the extent of 10 per cent, that is, in the above illustration at $55, we get reported net income of $25 and a 50 per cent compliance ratio. It will be observed from our tables that this is approximately what appears to have happened in our sample of landlords.

Table 2 shows the detail of the ultimate findings. It shows

Table 2
Summary of Gross and Net Rent Compliance

Type of unit	Number of cases	Ratio of reported gross rent to estimated gross rent	Ratio of reported net rent to estimated net rent
Multiple units	182	86.16	56.10
Rooms	62	68.24	25.39
Single units	47	66.46	48.06
Renter subletting	10	36.05	16.58
Garages	8	38.99	78.14
Total All cases	309	81.18	50.74

a ratio of aggregate reported to aggregate estimated net rent of nearly 51 per cent.

Two supplementary phases of the study may be noted briefly. A special analysis of expense items showed that errors in reporting these items are not general or uniform. The ratio of claimed to estimated expenses is relatively high for repairs and maintenance, furniture depreciation, equipment depreciation, and telephone expense. Several of the other items are modestly over-reported while two items, taxes and water, have estimated expenses (and in this case they are actual) larger than claimed expenses. Two expense items, repairs and maintenance, and depreciation, account for approximately 75 per cent of all the over-reporting of expenses and the item "repairs and maintenance" alone represents about 50 per cent of over-reporting. Landlords often depreciate both land and buildings and sometimes even adjoining lots.

An effort was also made to determine the tax-liability noncompliance in relation to proper tax compliance. For the major traffic (those reporting net income and rent) this was done in the aggregrate; that is, the average reported taxable income was determined along with the marginal rate at which incremental additions to that average income should be taxed. The average nonreported rental income was also determined along with the additional tax that would have been collected had this income been reported. To get a tax-compliance ratio one prorates the present tax between rental income and other income; also the proper tax between ascertained rental and other income (assuming the latter to be correct as stated). He then compares his two answers.[11] The tax-compliance record was found to be 47 per cent as compared with the net-rental-income-compliance ratio of nearly 51 per cent.

The above explanation omits the special treatment necessary for two types of taxpayers—the non-filers and filers not now liable to tax. The filers without tax liability were not numerous and were treated individually. The non-filers posed a problem and projection of a tax liability for them proved to be more a matter

[11] Thus if A has an income of $2,000 and reported rental income of $1,000 and a tax of $10, the tax on his rent is $5. If he should have reported $1,000 more in rent, his income should have been $3,000 and his tax perhaps $24. The hypothetical tax on his rent would be $16 and his compliance score 5 out of 16 or about 30 per cent.

of speculation than precise measurement. Nothing is finitely known about the income or exemption status of these landlords. The arbitrary assumptions were made that the net rental income for each case was equal to the sum of all other income received and that each landlord is entitled to two exemptions. The total effect of these assumptions is not crucial to the main conclusion.

One should beware of indicting all income-tax administration on the basis of any evidence here produced. Our study covers only one part of one kind of income in one area. Calculations based on national data indicate that personal-rent income in 1954 was less than 2.5 per cent of total personal income. Residential rent is one of the more difficult areas that income-tax administration is expected to police. However, it should not be too difficult to check rented properties, income from which goes entirely unreported. These could be ascertained from property-tax records. Some approximation of gross income could be calculated by inquiries as to unit-rent payments. Net rent would be much more difficult; here an inquiry or audit might be indicated if returns depart radically from well-established norms.

THE FIVE FINGER DISCOUNT*

MARY OWEN CAMERON

Every day in Chicago (where this study was made), or in any other large city, hundreds and possibly even thousands of people who have not so far been the subject of adequate criminological study commit larceny from retail merchants. Some are employees; some are shoplifters; some are professional thieves who specialize in taking merchandise from stockrooms and warehouses. The aggregate "take" of their theft is enormous. Twelve department stores in New York City, for example, collectively estimated as theft losses for the year 1951 about $10,000,000.[1] A store executive said in an interview, "If we actually knew what is being stolen we would probably lose our minds."

Loren Edwards, the former head of the store protection division of a large Chicago department store writes as follows:

"We lose more money by stock shortage than we make. . . ."
This statement, meaning that shrinkage was greater than profit, was made by a store comptroller at a comptroller's meeting.

* From Mary Owen Cameron, *The Booster and the Snitch: Department Store Shoplifting* (New York, Free Press of Glencoe, 1964).
[1] New York *Herald Tribune,* October 30, 1952.

Another store comptroller made the statement that "shoplifting in stores comprises 30% of all inventory shrinkage or loss." The theory has also been advanced that the major part of losses, due to theft, is caused by dishonest employees.

One expert in the field of shrinkage prevention has estimated that a fantastic sum of money—$1,700,000,000—is stolen from retailers each year. Another estimate was that approximately 100,000 thefts, at an average take of $15.00 each, are committed nationally each week. That figure would add up to $78,000,000 a year. In my opinion this is a very conservative figure.[2]

The reason for the great divergence in the "estimates" is to be found in department store and specialty store accounting practices: losses due to theft become part of a general, undifferentiated figure composed of several factors and known as "inventory shrinkage" or "inventory shortage." Inventory shrinkage is calculated by taking the difference between the retail price for merchandise, as assigned by store management, and the actual amount realized on the sale of the merchandise. It is usually reported as a per cent of gross sales volume. Thus a store with total receipts of $10,000,000 a year and an inventory shrinkage of $20,000 will calculate its loss as 2 per cent. In urban department store merchandising, a 2 per cent loss is generally considered a "good" figure. Some large department stores admit to shrinkage figures of 5 per cent or higher.

Inventory shrinkage is not wholly a result of theft. It may include losses due to price markdowns which occur when, for example, an item becomes shopworn or "dated" and is, at the discretion of a department manager, sold for less than the assigned price. Losses resulting from the disappearance of money or merchandise are also a part of inventory shrinkage. The word *disappearance* is used advisedly. It could possibly mean that the merchandise was "purchased" by a buyer but never really delivered to the store. A "paper deal" could have been contracted by a "responsible" employee.

In many departments of a large department store, price markdown clearly accounts for a smaller proportion of inven-

[2] Edwards, Loren, *Shoplifting and Shrinkage Protection for Stores* (Springfield, Ill., 1958), p. v.

tory shrinkage than theft; in other departments price markdown is presumed by the management to be a major component of inventory shrinkage.

Inventory shrinkage, then, is the index regularly used by merchants as a general measure for many forms of loss. Unfortunately, it is seldom a specific measure of theft and never a measure capable of differentiating between the different kinds of theft. Therefore it is impossible for store management, or anyone else, to specify accurately the amount of loss resulting from any particular component. Even if one is able to make some rough estimate of how much loss is due to theft and how much to markdown, it is impossible to give more than a semi-informed guess as to how much theft is the result of shoplifters and how much theft is the result of acts by employees.

Employee theft, it is generally agreed, is a large component, probably greater, perhaps much greater than shoplifting itself. Currently, store protection personnel speak of the "generally accepted" figure of 75 per cent of all theft as employee theft. Although this percentage may be "generally accepted," it is not, certainly, accurate. Some kinds of merchandise can be easily stolen by sales employees; some is more easily stolen from stockrooms and storage; still other merchandise is especially accessible to knowledgeable shoplifters. While a store with many departments may average out losses and arrive at a "generally accepted" figure, a specialty store's losses could run from zero to 100 per cent as a result of any possible component. Only a careful analysis of each department's or each store's particular problems can be useful in cutting the losses in that store or that department.

Store employees certainly have many opportunities to steal money, to carry out merchandise, or to pass merchandise on to confederates. The arrest of an employee for theft and a search of his lodgings often reveals large amounts of stolen merchandise, sometimes amounting to several thousands of dollars in value. The stolen merchandise recovered from the apartment of a teen-age boy who had worked in the camera section of a department store for six months included twenty suits, racks of neckties, forty-two cameras, and closets full of sheets, blankets, towels, shoes, underwear, cooking utensils, women's wear, etc. He had devised a not very foolproof but temporarily workable system of forging sales receipts with which his girl friend then obtained merchandise. Loren Edwards writes of this problem:

> Fidelity and surety companies have issued statements, at different times, estimating that employee dishonesty costs American business over a half billion dollars a year. These estimates usually cover fidelity losses that have been reported. It would be impossible to estimate the unknown amount of pilferage of merchandise from stores by employees.[3]

Donald Laird reports in *The Management Review*:[4]

> One eastern drug chain had a $1,400,000 inventory loss in six months so the management used lie detectors on its 1,400 employees. It was found that nearly three-fourths of the employees had been helping themselves to merchandise and petty cash. Such surveys seem to indicate that small-scale theft, cheating, lying, is prevalent in about 60% of the population.

Warehouse and stockroom theft may involve either employees or outsiders, and the operation of these thieves can cause large amounts of merchandise to disappear in a short period of time. There does not appear, however, to be any generally accepted estimate of the amount of loss resulting from this type of theft. One of the estimates is that of Norman Jaspan, President of Norman Jaspan Associates, who is quoted in the April 24, 1961 issue of *The Electrical Merchandising Week* as saying: "Over the years the cost of . . . malpractices by employees has been getting progressively greater until it has reached a total of $1,000,000,000 a year just in cash and goods." Jaspan's investigations, which he states were made over a period of 37 years, led him to believe that 70 per cent of inventory shortages were the result of employee malpractices; 25 per cent he believed were the result of honest clerical errors and the remainder a result of shoplifting. Japan's estimates for different merchandising units were as follows:

[3] *Ibid.*, p. 61.
[4] "Psychology and the Crooked Employee," *The Management Review,* April, 1950.

Type of Store	Total $ value of sales	Loss resulting from employee dishonesty
Department stores	16,000,000,000	140,000,000
Supermarkets	50,000,000,000	100,000,000
Hardware stores	9,000,000,000	90,000,000
Discount houses	4,500,000,000	25,000,000
Variety stores	4,000,000,000	60,000,000
Drug retailers	6,000,000,000	50,000,000
Others	135,000,000,000	140,000,000

Jaspan attributed the majority of these losses to employees at supervisory levels.

E. B. Weiss, writing in the December, 1958 issue of *Advertising Age,* also argued that shoplifting is a minor factor: "If shopper pilferage were totally eliminated it would hardly make a dent in the total shortage factor! . . . Store employees of all ranks out-steal the shopper."

He called for a "deep study of shopper pilferage."

Perhaps some day the great manufacturing associations in food, drug, soft and hard goods will come together and underwrite a study to be made by a competent firm of auditors-investigators. I am positive that statistics will leave not the slightest doubt that the real culprit in stock shortages is not the shopper—but the retailer, his policies and practices, and his staff.

He believed that many retail merchants indulge in the luxury of poor control, poor personnel practices, and poor accounting practices. Mr. Weiss noted that one department store with an annual turnover of about $17,000,000 reported stock shortage of 1.3 per cent. When a more competent audit was made, losses were, in fact, 2.9 per cent. In housewares losses were 9 per cent and in cosmetics 5 per cent.

Impressions gathered in the course of the present study also support the view that employee theft far outranks shoplifting as a source of loss to retail merchants. Be this as it may, shoplifting is still a considerable source of loss, and more important from the point of view of this study, a major form of crime. How *major* has been obscured by the fact that it is handled by private rather than public police. As a result, arrests for shoplifting (or of employees for stealing) seldom come to the public attention and seldom become part of the public records which form the basis for most crime statistics.

Detectives employed by a single downtown department store in Chicago, for example, arrested two-thirds as many adult women for shoplifting in that store in 1944 and again in 1945 as those shown in the official statistics on larceny as being formally charged by the police with petty larceny of all forms (including shoplifting) in the entire city of Chicago. This figure becomes even more impressive if one assumes store detectives are correct in believing that perhaps they apprehend only about one person out of every ten who shoplift on any particular day.

HANDLING THE SHOPLIFTING PROBLEM

Since so little has been written in the serious literature of criminology about shoplifting, and since such erroneous impressions are gained from folklore and popular literature on the subject, some description of this form of larceny as it exists in actual practice must be presented at the outset. Information for this presentation has been acquired mainly in conversation with retail merchants and managers of retail chain stores.

Throughout any urban area, retail store owners or managers realize from time to time that certain items of merchandise are unaccountably missing. When a storekeeper, for instance, believes that losses are especially heavy, he may keep track of particular objects and discover to his dismay that of a dozen toothbrushes or cigarette lighters that were placed on display, six remain, two were sold, and four are gone and unaccounted for. All kinds of merchandise, from toys to television sets disappear. Occasionally the merchant sees someone steal an item. His reaction then depends on himself and the thief. There is no standardized way of meeting the situation, but the one thing the merchant seldom does is to call the police.

Independent merchants empirically develop their own methods of dealing with shoplifters. One grocer said that when he sees an adult lifting something, he adds $5 to the grocery bill. When the thief asks, "What is this?" the grocer answers significantly, "You know." And he suggests that perhaps the "customer" would rather leave and do his shopping elsewhere. A druggist reported that he always asks to wrap *the rest* of the "customer's" merchandise, pointedly emphasizing the words. If the thief fails to produce the stolen merchandise, the druggist says emphatically, "I'll keep *you* in mind." A hardware retailer reported that he uses the direct approach, "Look, I got eyes. You took two paring knives. Pay me for them."

The manager of a large bookstore in New York reported that while the store personnel never arrest a shoplifter, sales clerks are instructed to "breathe down the neck" of anyone suspected of stealing. A suspected thief is watched so carefully—even obviously—that he goes away.

Most independent merchants seem to believe that after having once tactfully let a thief know that he has been "spotted," he will never return to the store.

Larger merchandising enterprises, chain grocery, drug, variety stores, appliance shops and the like usually follow the same system of dealing with shoplifters as do small independent retailers. When a clerk sees merchandise being stolen, he is usually instructed to notify the manager who personally "suggests" to the thief that the merchandise be paid for or returned. In a chain store in which inventory shrinkage exceeds an allotted limit, private detectives may be called in to arrest some of the offenders and occasionally formal charges of arrest are placed against shoplifters.

In some branches of retail merchandising, on the other hand, store protection officials admit ruefully that inventory shortage is no problem. One large chain of bookdealers reported less than .5 per cent loss. Instead of regarding this minuscule loss as a cause for rejoicing, it was regarded as the result of "old fashioned" merchandising methods including much personal service by a large staff of sales clerks. "Certainly," said the security representative, "we have a small inventory shortage, but our payroll for sales personnel cuts our profit to almost nothing. We could be ahead by accepting the inevitability of shoplifting. Self-service plus all the losses it will bring will net us more profit in the long run than individualized service with almost no loss at all."

As compared with retail booksellers, it is worth noting, public libraries (with books on supermarket-type open shelves in the privacy of stacks and with almost no security precautions) have only minor pilferage problems. One large urban library system reported that its losses in all forms of pilferage (failure of borrowers to return books, theft from open stacks, etc.) represented less than 1 per cent of its holdings for circulation (and less than .05 per cent of its actual circulation).

But the trend toward self-service supermarkets in the retail grocery business, as well as in other retail merchandising, in the last two decades has made "foodlifting" a fairly profitable field attracting even "professional" shoplifters. Food store detectives tell of thieves carrying out a dozen steaks at a time or large quantities of canned fish, turkey, or other "fancy" goods.[5]

Retail trade journals indicate an increasing concern with shoplifting in stores that deal in specialized items: phonographs, tape recorders, records, electric shavers, cameras, and camera supplies. In many of these stores modern merchandising methods relying on self-service have cut the sales staff, but in some types of retail sales a substantial part of the resulting saving has been absorbed by inventory shrinkage. As self-service rises, store personnel increasingly find themselves at a loss for methods of dealing with theft.

Just as in the past when safe manufacturers and safe crackers ran a seesaw race for what resulted in a now virtually crackproof safe, manufacturers and thieves have turned to a duel over the packaging of goods. A symposium in the August, 1959 issue of *Modern Packaging* recommends measures to reduce pilferage. Multiple packaging, i.e., putting six bars of soap into a single bag reduces the likelihood of pilferage. One bar of soap is easily slipped into a pocket—not so, six. Wrapping fresh fruit will prevent the housewife from selecting the top layer of strawberries from each pint box and making up a box of her own with nothing but top-grade berries (the exact nature of the dishonesty involved here may escape most housewives and readers). Gluing small packages such as razor blades on outsized cards will prevent their pilferage. In fact, a survey by Pax Fax Inc. (reported in the article above) found that, regardless of value, merchandise in small packages was more often pilfered than the same merchandise wrapped in or glued to large packages.

Other supermarket "tricks" of pilferers include filling the deceptively large boxes of soap flakes or cereal to the brim from

[5] For an interesting descriptive article on "foodlifting," see Bill Fay (of the Jewel Food Company in Chicago), "I Am a Supermarket Detective," *Collier's*, March 29, 1952.

other boxes, and switching caps (on which prices are stamped) of small bottles of hand lotion or shampoo to large bottles having the same size cap. Dave Chapman, a leading packager, says, "The philosophy of self-service and open-rack merchandising is predicated on the increase in sales appeal by removing the inhibitants between the consumer and the product. The closer we get the consumer to the product, the higher the chance he will buy." [6] The higher the chance, too, that he will steal.

The trade journals of camera and phonographic supply organizations report that shoplifters are "taking everything that isn't nailed down." Transistor radios, tape recorders, and small TV sets as well as cameras, film, audio tape, and records can "be kissed goodbye" if they are unattended for a moment. The trend toward miniaturization of equipment for audio and visual recording is of great help to the thief. Characteristically these equipment shops turn to more equipment as an answer to theft —protection equipment. Trade journals advertise closed-circuit TV installations to discourage pilfering and frequently store managers work out ways to hook all display models of small radios, TV's, and the like to a single circuit which, when broken by the removal of any one set, sounds an alarm. One such protection device sells for $15 and is the size of a cigar box. Mounted on an electrical wall outlet, demonstrator sets are plugged into it. If the plug of a radio is pulled out, a light or a buzzer is set off.

Convex, regular, and "one way" mirrors are used by many retail merchants to keep their stock under observation from a distance or from around corners. For remote alcoves in specialty shops invisible infrared circuits can be set up to warn sales personnel that someone has entered the alcove. Customers are also often asked to check their briefcases and shopping bags. For the legitimate customer, this can sometimes be made to seem a service; the potential shoplifter who refuses to check his luggage is thus more easily recognized.

Even in the most modern retail bookstores valuable art books are still kept behind counters, as much, however, to protect the books from vandalism as from theft. Books on sex and marriage "simply walk off" unless they are kept in locked cases. "Perhaps," a store manager hazarded, "people are embarrassed to buy these

[6] *Modern Packaging*, August, 1959.

books. Theft may seem a less difficult means of acquiring them."

But once a shoplifter is detected, all stores face the same problem of knowing how to deal with him. Children who pilfer are often treated more severely and directly than adults. They are usually scolded, their names recorded, and their parents notified. They may be warned not to come into the store again and threatened with police action if they do.

The caution with which adult shoplifters must be treated and the more severe treatment accorded children reflect a general problem that confronts the shoplifting victim. Whether he is a small owner-merchant, the store manager of a nationwide retail chain, or a store detective, in dealing with adults the victim must understand the law of arrest if he is, in fact, going to stop or arrest a thief.

Technically and legally any citizen who sees a crime being committed, whether felony or misdemeanor, has the right and, indeed, the obligation to halt (arrest) the criminal or to assist in his arrest. In exercising this right, however, the citizen must be certain that he observes the proper legal forms. He may otherwise be committing an act of false arrest.

In the common law, the power of arrest resided almost equally in the police and the ordinary citizen. The legal right of arrest was as follows: Arrests could be made on warrants, or written orders of the court, by anyone authorized to serve them. Arrests could be made without such warrants on two conditions: (a) that a crime was known to have been committed and (b) that the crime was committed in the presence of the person making the arrest, or, in case the crime was a felony and was not committed in the presence of the arresting officer, he had good reason to suspect that the person arrested was guilty. That is, a person committing a misdemeanor could not be arrested, except on warrant, by anyone, police officer or other, not present when the offense was being committed; a person suspected of having committed a felony might be arrested by one who was not present when the felony was committed, provided he had positive knowledge that a felony had been committed by someone and had good reason to suspect that this was the guilty person. This is the general law of arrest, which has been modified somewhat by statutes.[7]

[7] Sutherland, Edwin H., *Principles of Criminology* (Philadelphia, 1939), pp. 233–234.

False arrest, slander, forcible detention, and even kidnaping charges can be instituted against a person who makes a citizen arrest. This is not a problem equally faced by the public police who are relatively immune to civil suits for damages. In a citizen arrest, when direct accusation is made, the store owner, manager, or owner's representative may become involved in an expensive and time-consuming lawsuit. Should the owner or his employee have made an error, albeit an honest error, or for any reason be unable to prove the charge, there might be heavy damages to pay to the arrested person. A defense attorney may make the charge quite difficult to prove since the arresting citizen seldom knows adequately the laws of evidence. For two paring knives or a package of candy, or even for more expensive items, the merchant often reasons, the risk is not worth taking.*

In Illinois, prior to the shoplifting law effective in 1957 (subsequent to the time the arrests studied here were made), a merchant or his representative faced the danger of a lawsuit for false arrest if he detained an innocent person. This remains the common practice in most states. Edwards writes:

In case of arrest or detention it was necessary to prove to a court or a jury that a crime actually had been committed in the presence of the arrester, and that the arrested person was guilty. Failure to do this, and if prosecution should fail, the merchant could be liable for false arrest or false imprisonment, and be required to pay civil damages. For this reason, some merchants, including nationally known retail organizations, took no action against shoplifters.

The laws of many of the states similarly restrict merchants in the protection of their property; however some states recognize a middle ground which can be used as a partial solution to the shoplifting problem, while at the same time preserving the rights of a person arrested.

This middle ground allows a merchant to detain a person if he

* Although clarity for the reader might call for the use of separate words to indicate "store arrest" or "citizen arrest" *v.* official police arrest, the word "arrest" has been chosen deliberately for both kinds of arrest, and distinctions will be made by the adjective when these distinctions are necessary and not already clear from the context. In either case a thief is "arrested" or stopped in the act of larceny and the arresting citizen or officer must have seen the offender commit the offense. Citizen or police officer, he must be prepared to testify to this in court.

has probable cause, not mere suspicion, for believing that the person detained has unlawfully appropriated merchandise. The detention must be limited to a reasonable time.[8]

Most states are more strict. An Ohio appellate court even had to rule that the actions of a store manager did not amount to false arrest when he approached a customer and said, "Madam, that bag will have to be searched." The court ruled that the defendant company

thought its private right to property was being violated, which it was resisting. It was not assuming to vindicate any public right. The plaintiff was not accused of any crime. Nothing was done to indicate that she was being held for delivery to a peace officer to answer criminal charge. Under such circumstances there is no basis for the suggestion that this is a false imprisonment, indicated by false arrest. [Lester v. Albers Super Markets. *Ohio Appeals 114 N.E.* (2) 529, 1952, p. 532.]

Only rarely in relation to the total number of arrests for shoplifting by private police do public police make arrests other than "technical" bookings made on the complaint of store personnel. The main functions of the "store detail" of an urban detective force are to trace professional shoplifting troupes and their "fences"; and to convey persons already arrested by private police to a place of confinement prior to their establishing bail.

Of the many adults and children who commit larceny by shoplifting on any particular day, only a few are actually seen. Of those who are seen, many are handled by implied threat. Only a few shoplifters, seen by store managers actually taking especially valuable merchandise or those who are seen by private detectives, are ever arrested. Of the number arrested by citizen arrest (and this includes arrests made by private detectives), only an unknown proportion (store officials estimate between 10 per cent and 35 per cent) are prosecuted and thus have their records incorporated into official criminal statistics. Shoplifters who are not caught, of course, and those who are "caught" but not arrested by store managements, form an un-

[8] Edwards, *op. cit.*, p. 176.

known and actually unknowable segment of the criminal—or quasi-criminal—population.

PEOPLE WHO BECOME "DATA"

The present study presents an analysis (largely from statistical evidence) of two main samples of the "knowable" class of shoplifters. The first segment of data consists of a sample (called the "Store" sample) of one out of four of the shoplifters arrested by detectives of one department store in the eight-year period 1943–1950. The department store from which this sample of arrests is used will be referred to as the Store (capital "S") or Lakeside Co. Department stores are naturally reluctant to have this punitive phase of their activity become the subject of public discussion, but the validity of the results is in no way affected by the anonymity of the Store. Disguising the name, as is done in this case, is no different in principle from the usual practice of eliminating or disguising names in case history reports.

The second major sample of shoplifting arrests used in this study (called the "Women's Court" sample) is composed of the adult women who were seen, arrested, and *formally charged* with "petty larceny, shoplifting" by all the stores in the city of Chicago for the three-year period 1948–1950. Some data on men arrested for shoplifting and prosecuted in the Municipal Court were also obtained, and some information taken from police arrest records of shoplifters is given.

Although these data, coming as they do from specific (and available) sources, cannot be taken as representative of the total group of shoplifters, they nevertheless form the most adequate data so far available on shoplifting.

Since one of the major objectives of this study will be the analysis of factors which bias the statistical records of both "Store" and "court" samples (an objective which can best be realized as the records are themselves presented), there will be little attempt to discuss biasing factors prior to the presentation of the data. It seems useful, however, to make an exception in regard to the "place bias" already touched upon (those shoplifters who happen to steal at stores employing detectives are almost the only ones arrested) and to emphasize the range and variety of selective factors that bring about the arrest of a shoplifter and perhaps bring him to official attention.

Aside from stealing at a store in which arrests are made by managers, proprietors, or private police, in order to be apprehended, the shoplifter must also come under the direct observation of the arresting person. Even when closed-circuit television is used, the person who steals one object and is observed on the television screen must usually be followed by a detective until he steals another article while under the direct observation of the detective. (Although, as noted above, the laws of arrest differ markedly in different states.) The risk to store management of being deliberately "framed" into a "false" arrest by the thief is always present. The risk to the store varies in accordance with the social status of the offender. The apparent marks of social status (dress, grooming, age, race, etc.) influence the detectives or store managers who must file the formal charge of arrest.

Detectives must see the act of shoplifting take place in order to make an arrest, and detectives cannot be equally observant of all persons in the store. (In some department stores, Lakeside Co. among them, sales clerks are rewarded by the management for "tips" to detectives on thieves, but the proportion of shoplifters arrested as a result of such tips is low—12 per cent for Lakeside Co. Actually, the chief objective of the tip procedure is not to detect shoplifters but to use employees to detect fellow employees who commit violations of trust, including stealing merchandise.)

Shoplifters arrested by store detectives, then, are usually persons who are deliberately watched or those the detectives "just happen" to see. Since the detectives' methods of operation determine who will be arrested, the question of the types of person they are "likely to see" is of considerable importance.

In department stores the detectives are mainly women. On duty they wear hats and coats, carry handbags and try to look like typical shoppers. Detectives are distributed one or two to a floor or section in the large stores (except for sections that are devoted to furniture, carpets, yard goods, and other relatively "non-shopliftable" merchandise).

Detectives frequently have duties to perform that involve the safety of staff and customers as well as the protection of merchandise; they are not engaged solely for the detection of shoplifters. If a lighted match is carelessly or deliberately thrown into a trash bin and a fire results, the store protection person is summoned by the sales clerk. If an elevator fails to function or an escalator becomes jammed, the first person on the scene will usually be "store protection." If a heart attack, fainting spell, or epileptic seizure occurs, among customers or employees, the call goes to store protection immediately. Or when customers quarrel and fight over a bargain, "I saw it first," store protection enters the scene to calm upset tempers. The efficient store detective, too, knows that any one of these emergencies may have been created for the purpose of taking him away from what could soon be the scene of a crime. An immediate call for help goes to the central office to bring other store detectives to the spot.

The chief "first floor" operator in a large urban store stated that in one month she and her assistants encountered alcoholics and narcotics addicts dashing in to steal merchandise. They also helped a person who had wandered into the store and collapsed as a result of a concussion following an automobile accident outside the store. A man was seen indecently exposing himself. And a fatal heart attack occurred. Along with these events, shoplifting, purse-snatching, and pocket-picking continued.

Store detectives are somewhat free to move about and to station themselves wherever experience has shown they will be most successful in their multitudinous assignments. On a floor where costume jewelry is displayed, for example, a detective frequently stands at the counter. While apparently just another customer also trying on jewelry, she is actually watching for someone to "pocket" or to put on and wear something away. She will be particularly attentive when merchandise falls or is pushed onto the floor, for this is done intentionally by thieves so that they can be concealed from the clerks while hiding merchandise in a shopping bag or a handbag. When a shoplifter is seen concealing merchandise or leaving the counter with it, he (or she) will be followed from the department and perhaps from the store before being arrested. For relatively inexpensive items, the thief will probably not be arrested then but will be followed. If a single object of small value is the only theft, the thief may even be allowed to leave the store without being arrested. The danger of error in arrest, and the hazards of deliberate enticement into making false arrests, are, comparatively, too great to risk arresting a person who has stolen only an inexpensive piece of merchandise.

A man, for example, was observed by the writer and a store detective pocketing a snakeskin billfold valued at $24. The store detective, who observed the man acting very suspiciously and conspicuously, did not arrest him. She had observed that he wore a "trench coat" which undoubtedly had doublepocket openings leading to his suit pockets or to the floor. She assumed, correctly it appeared later, that the thief's motivation was to be arrested after having "thrown" the merchandise (kicked the billfold into an inconspicuous corner). Perhaps he would have resisted arrest and forced the detective to injure him (such cases have occurred before) in the arrest proceedings. He might even have stationed seemingly reputable witnesses in strategic locations to observe the damage inflicted upon him. He could therefore become the plaintiff in a suit for large damages from the store. In this particular case, at least, the store detective pointed out that the thief had indeed "thrown" the stolen billfold by the simple expedient of placing it between his sets of pockets and allowing it to fall to the floor. If captured, there would be no evidence of stolen merchandise on his person: he would have seemed to be an innocent victim of an over-enthusiastic store detective and the store would have been the victim of a cleverly arranged suit for false arrest.

An experienced store detective made the interesting observation that most thieves once they are outside of the store and believe themselves beyond the range of observation of store detectives remove the stolen merchandise from parcels or pockets and examine it. When this examination takes place on a street corner or on a public conveyance, as it frequently does, the detective who has followed the thief then makes his arrest. If the thief proceeds to the privacy of his own home without showing incriminating evidence, he has less likelihood of being caught.

In sections of a department store where the technique is applicable, and especially for the "gift" departments during the Christmas season, one-way mirrors and peep holes (through which, in either case, the operator can see without being seen) may make up a part of the ornamentation. The usefulness of this technique, however, is limited, as is closed-circuit television. In order to arrest a shoplifter who has been seen stealing merchandise, the operator behind the mirror must either have some way of signaling to another on the floor, or the operator must let the shoplifter out of his sight for the period of time it takes him to get from his hiding place to the shoplifter. This is undesirable since the thief may, during this time, have changed his mind, or passed the merchandise to a confederate or may deliberately have "thrown" the merchandise to invite false arrest.

In departments where especially valuable items are displayed: fur coats, silver, cameras, luggage, etc., operators may be especially stationed to guard these things. There they often function best by looking, to the initiated, conspicuously like plain-clothes detectives or they may even wear uniforms. One detective to whom I was introduced—she looked like an unflattering stereotype of a prison matron or a female "cop"—said that she had been "in furs" for six years. "No," she said, "I've never arrested anyone. I just come here every day and either sit where people can see me or just walk around and look at people suspiciously. The insurance company requires a guard, and I'm it."

Many stores station uniformed police at exits. Again their service is prevention and assistance in arrest rather than detection.

Aside from watching merchandise being handled by customers, operators follow and observe "likely" suspects. They develop, they believe, after years of experience on their job, a "sixth sense" for people who are intending to steal. Certain mannerisms of the shoplifter are sometimes clues. The typical shopper looks at merchandise and ignores other people in the store; the shoplifter constantly watches people in order to know whether or not he is being observed or followed. When the store detective observes a "customer" looking at people rather than merchandise, he may follow the person, unobtrusively of course, through the store. Among other specific clues that the store detectives look for are shopping bags, knitting bags, briefcases, large purses, etc., within which merchandise may be concealed. Large bags with the store label (hat bags and the like) that appear to be crinkled or to have been folded and refolded may have been acquired by shoplifters and kept for shoplifting tours. Persons with such "luggage" are carefully observed. Detectives also look for signs of tension and strain.

Another group of people considered "likely" suspects and watched by most department store detectives are unaccompanied adolescents. In many stores adolescent groups are under almost constant observation, and this practice, according to detectives, proves worthwhile. It is also a distorting factor in statistical generalizations that involve frequency of arrest.

Negro people are also kept under much closer observation than whites. It is clear that here, too, the selective observations of store detectives constitute a source for distortion of arrest statistics. One cannot measure this bias nor the bias against adolescents and evaluate its importance by any objective standard, but it is unquestionably present and is a factor of some significance in influencing the selection of persons to be arrested. Racial bias is general and not especially characteristic of any particular store. Operators who have worked in several stores and in different cities have the same outlook and the same prejudices. Shoplifters who blend into the dominant group of shoppers are less likely to be noticed. The woman shoplifter who appears to be well-to-do and carries herself with poise and assurance is least likely to be observed, or apprehended even if she is observed. A detective must be very sure of his evidence before he risks the arrest of someone he believes to have no prior criminal record, or possibly may have connections in high places, and be able to obtain first-rate legal counsel.

To summarize, the distorting factors in arrest statistics that have been touched on so far have included five points: Some stores employ detectives empowered to make arrests and others do not; the stationing and operating methods of detectives employed by stores influence what they see being stolen; the anti-Negro attitude of many detectives increases the chance of their seeing Negro shoplifters; adolescents are more frequently under observation than adults; and finally, the caution the store detective feels he must exercise in arresting anyone is enhanced when the suspected thief appears to be "respectable."

These distorting factors probably apply generally to all stores as well as department stores. They operate to select out of the general run of shoplifters those who will have any action taken against them. They are, in a sense, accidental or unconscious selective factors. But in the step which occurs between store arrest, once made, and court procedure, selective screening is deliberately and consciously introduced.

When inventory shrinkage is particularly high, store officials announce, sometimes stridently, that all apprehended shoplifters will be prosecuted. They may even post signs to this effect. They believe that "word gets around" and that shoplifters will go elsewhere. These assertions are not, however, to be taken at face value.

Store police cannot formally charge all persons who are arrested. Since testimony in court takes up the time of store detectives, department store staff generally wish to prosecute as few arrested persons as possible. The problem is much the same for stores everywhere.

It will surprise people to learn that one important London store lost between £15,000 and £21,000 last year through petty pilfering. . . . Arrests are made but few thieves are charged, for when a summons is issued the head of the department involved and at least one of his assistants, must attend the court, which means the staff is shorthanded for several days. An average of twenty thieves are caught weekly in a large department store and were all charged, the directors would be faced with a total of at least 1,040 court cases a year. Suppose it were decided to proceed in all these cases and suppose an average of two witnesses were needed on each charge, and suppose in each case only two days were needed on each charge, and suppose in each case only two witnesses were needed, the firm would still lose 4,160 working days in the year. It is obvious that under these circumstances no firm can afford to push a campaign against the shoplifter.[9]

In the Chicago Municipal Court, a misdemeanant court, procedures are somewhat less time-consuming than in the British court described by Cecil Bishop. But if the defendant demands, as he may, a jury trial, or if he obtains continuances of his case, several man-days of detectives' time may be wasted, from the store viewpoint, in court. Even a routine case requires at least half a day of detectives' time.

[9] Bishop, Cecil, *Women and Crime* (London, 1931), pp. 6–7.

All large stores, then, face the problem of who among those who have been caught is to be prosecuted. The actual method of selection, however, is, in some degree, arbitrary and "intuitional." The store protection official who is judge of this process acts on an individual basis and without following any necessary rules of precedence. A social worker at the Chicago Municipal Court said that after twenty years' experience of seeing shoplifters being tried, she had yet to discover any principles underlying what appeared to be "sheer caprice" on the part of department store staffs. "Sometimes," she said, "one store will have its detectives in court testifying every day of the week. And another time only a few well-known professionals will be brought in."

Although "sheer caprice" may have some hand in the selective screening procedure, some general principlés operate also. Individuals are screened within a context which makes it desirable to prosecute as few persons as possible and still to protect merchandise from theft and the store from suits for false arrest. In determining whether or not a person is to be formally charged or released without charge, store officials look at two different problems: they wish to prosecute thieves who are shoplifting commercially, and they need to obtain a conviction in court.

If the arrested shoplifter is likely to be a person stealing merchandise in order to sell it or to return it for refund of the "purchase" price, he is almost certain to be formally charged. The evidence pointing toward "commercial" theft that interrogators look for includes a catalogue of items such as inadequate or inaccurate personal identification. A thief may carry a driver's license or other identifying documents belonging to someone whose pocket he has picked earlier in the day. Failure of the thief to live up to all aspects of his "identification" is cause for further interrogation at the very least. The thief who gives an out-of-town address or a hotel address may well be a *professional* thief. Pawn tickets, keys to public lockers, and the like are sure to be followed through by a thorough search of the places indicated before the shoplifter is allowed to walk out of the store. The nature and value of the stolen merchandise and special equipment for stealing or concealing merchandise is considered in determining whether the detective is confronted with commercial theft. Store detectives also observe the thief's behavior during the time he is being followed. They know that an experienced thief, having stolen merchandise of value, will often go *up* an escalator rather than immediately *down* and out of the store. The thief will discover in this way whether or not he is being followed. He will also try to find a place where he can conceal himself and remove price tags or other incriminating labels. Staircases, rest rooms, and telephone booths are usually the most available places; hence they are watched with some care. Store detectives also look for narcotics addiction as evidenced by behavior, by needle marks, or by the possession of narcotics.

While it is clearly in the interest of department stores to prosecute commercial shoplifters, they must also have a voluntary statement or a court finding of guilt for every arrested person. Those who refuse to sign a confession and a waiver of suit against the store must be prosecuted in the court. Only when a shoplifter has signed a confession of guilt—or has been found guilty by the court—is the store free from suit for false arrest. Although a shoplifter may be an obvious novice, he must still be prosecuted if he refuses to absolve the store from guilt in apprehending him.

Aside from protective and financial considerations, other factors sometimes influence the decision to prosecute or release. Occasionally, for instance, prosecution is used as a means of getting a severely disturbed neurotic or psychotic person to a source of adequate medical care. The court can, and sometimes does, refer arrested persons to the psychiatric division.

The overall number of formal charges made by a particular store may be subject to considerable variation. The formal arrest rate will increase, for instance, if the store management becomes worried about the problem of inventory shrinkage and adopts a "get tough" policy for a period of time. There are also variations between stores. Store officials differ in the proportion of persons they feel it desirable to charge formally. "Sheer caprice" may play a part. Since knowledge of prosecution policy is not something store officials desire to make public, they discuss the problems involved with an outsider only with the understanding that they will not be quoted. Enough information was gathered in interviews with protection officials of stores in several cities, however, to make it seem likely that, among department stores, "class" stores generally prefer charges against a smaller proportion of arrested persons than do "mass" stores. Store detectives who have worked in both types of stores agreed with this generalization.

Prosecution policy of "mass" stores requires less emphasis on screening. Persons who shoplift in "mass" stores are already somewhat self-selected for lower social class status, and the likelihood of a prominent individual or his wife entering a "not guilty" plea and being found so by the court is therefore not as great as in the "class" stores.

THE CORPORATE AND JUDICIAL DISPOSITION
OF EMPLOYEE THIEVES *

GERALD D. ROBIN

The findings and discussion presented in this paper are based upon an empirical analysis of occupational crimes committed by department store employees against their employers.** Three large, independent department store companies (hereafter referred to as Company A, B, and C) provided the source data utilized in the study. The population examined consisted of the confidential security records of all employees who committed crimes against their firms and who were apprehended (1) from 1959 through 1962 in Company A, (2) from 1949 through 1963 in Company B, and (3) from 1956 through 1963 in Company C.[1]

* From Gerald D. Robin, "The Corporate and Judicial Disposition of Employee Thieves," *Wisconsin Law Review,* 685 (1967).
** This paper is part of a larger study which was supported by the National Institute of Mental Health in the form of a Research Fellowship.
[1] The cases included within these time periods comprised the companies' entire recorded experience on apprehended dishonest employees that was available when the writer began collecting the data. Since the collection of data was begun in the latter part of 1963 in Company A, it was obviously impossible to include all of their 1963 employee cases in the study. Moreover, since many of Company A's 1963 dishonest employee records which were "available" were still being processed by the office staff and were therefore incomplete, it was decided to exclude them entirely.

The number of cases of such dishonest employees constituting the individual populations was 739, 584, and 358 in Company A, B, and C, respectively—a total of 1681 dishonest employees.

The Department Store Study offered an unusual opportunity to investigate empirically the role assumed by an organized private sector—in this case, Big Business—in the treatment of offenders, to make some observations and inferences concerning the social factors which influence the sentencing behavior of judges, and to reflect upon the integration of private v. official conceptions of justice and its implementation.

Upon taking a dishonest employee into custody, the first and most important objective of the company is to obtain a signed confession from the suspect. In the process other information—reasons for stealing, whether others were involved, how, how often, and how long the offender had been embezzling, amount taken, etc.—were elicited with varying frequency. Of the 1662 cases for A–C (Companies A, B, and C combined [2]) in which the embezzlers' reaction to apprehension was known, 85 per cent signed a confession and another 3 per cent verbally admitted their guilt but refused to sign a statement to that effect; only 12 per cent flatly denied stealing, although many of these admitted to "violations of store policy." Ninety-three per cent of the trust violators in Company A confessed their guilt (90% signed a statement) compared with 87 per cent in Company B (86% signed a statement) and only 78 per cent in Company C (75% signed a statement).

The initial response of most of the offenders during interrogation was some form of denial: anger, shock, indignation, silence. However, as the questioning continued and the case against them was developed, they ultimately "broke down" and confessed their thefts, often becoming repentant while pleading, "I realize what a terrible thing I have done and it will never happen again." With regard to such promises of atonement they are unwittingly prophetic, since—as will be brought out shortly—the company

[2] The abbreviation "Co. A–C" or any variation thereof, such as Companies A–C, A–C combined, etc., refers to findings based upon and which apply to the trust violators of all three companies combined. If the sentence or context of the paragraph does not make clear the company for which the results are being reported, the reader should assume that they refer to all three companies combined.

does not give them the opportunity to repeat the mistake. In any event, many of the embezzlers are visibly affected by being discovered and confronted with the fact of their criminal behavior and apparently are more concerned that their conduct be concealed from "relevant" others, *i.e.,* with the effect of social degradation, than with the possibility of prosecution and imprisonment per se.

DISPOSITION BY THE COMPANY

The company has three courses of action open with respect to the final disposition of the offender: dismissal without prosecution (release), dismissal and prosecution, or retention of the employee. Two hundred eighty-eight of the 1681 trust violators in Companies A–C, or 17 per cent, were prosecuted. Eight dishonest employees were retained, 2 in Company B who had been recommended for employment by a very high official in the organization and who were therefore given a second chance, and 6 in Company C for reasons unknown to the researcher. (None of the employees were prosecuted *and* retained.) Apprehension for department store trust violation, then, results in automatic discharge but only infrequently in prosecution.

The overall prosecution rate of 17 per cent conceals important differences in attitude toward the disposition of thieving employees by Companies B and C on the one hand, and Company A on the other: 2 per cent of the 584 offenders and 8 per cent of the 358 offenders in the former companies, respectively, were prosecuted, compared with a surprisingly large prosecution rate of 34 per cent in the latter company. In addition, 32 Company A employees who were not prosecuted were turned over to the military or juvenile authorities, thus raising to almost two-fifths (38%) the proportion of offenders against whom some official action was taken. Differences this large are not fortuitous but rather reflect basic policy differences between Companies B and C and Company A concerning prosecution. Companies B and C were much more interested in terminating dishonest employee cases as quickly as possible, were more sympathetic toward their employees who had violated their trust, felt that prosecution generally served no useful purpose from their point of view and wished to avoid any further publicity in an admittedly sensitive area. By contrast, Company A's position was that criminal behavior on the part of their workers—biting the hand that feeds them—should result in observable punitive consequences extending beyond loss of employment whenever possible. Whereas management's philosophy in Companies B and C precluded prosecution a priori except in a small minority of the most exceptional cases, the security department in Company A had to justify to its management *not* prosecuting a dishonest employee. Of course, even in Company A, 2 out of every 3 trust violators were not prosecuted but presumably—and this area will be explored in a following section—this was primarily a matter of economics. The writer is convinced that the attitude of Company A toward prosecution is exceptional among department store organizations: the officials of six department store companies not part of the present study indicated in interviews with the researcher that they prosecute 5 to 10 per cent of their apprehended dishonest employees. Therefore, legal action against dishonest department store employees as an occupational group must be considered minimal, despite the unique attitude of Company A. As is true of white-collar crime, in employee theft the penal sanctions against criminal behavior have differential and selective implementation.[3] In Companies B and C combined, the proportion of trust violators who were prosecuted (4%) was almost identical with that in black market cases of price, rationing, and rent violations in which criminal proceedings were initiated (6%).[4]

While there is general agreement among informed students of the subject that, given the condition of sporadic law-enforcement, the major deterrent to trust violation is the fear of loss of position and social degradation through exposure, the deterrent effect of prosecution is debatable. Hall guardedly suggests that Post Office experience, and to some extent that of banks, indicates that efficient enforcement of the law deters embezzlement.[5] Offenses committed by Post Office workers are invariably reported to the United States District Attorney, who is charged with making the decision concerning prosecution; but at least every case is reported to the proper official and the policy of the

[3] Vilheim Aubert, "White Collar Crime and Social Structure," *American Journal of Sociology* 58 (November, 1952), p. 265.
[4] Marshall B. Clinard, *The Black Market* (New York: Rinehart & Company, Inc., 1952), pp. 33, 237–238.
[5] Hall, *loc. cit.*, p. 333.

Post Office is to support prosecution[6]—unlike department stores in general, Companies B and C in particular and, to a lesser extent, even Company A. At least 87 per cent of the 2,017 offenders who embezzled or committed related defalcations in insured non-member banks from 1935 through 1950 were prosecuted.[7] In contrast to these situations there was a virtual absence of law-enforcement in Companies B and C and non-prosecution not as a rule but as a reality in Company A in over half the cases. At the same time, the rate of apprehended postal dishonest employees is 1.4 per 1,000 workers[*] compared with an annual rate of 4.8 employees in Companies A–C. The fact that the annual rate of apprehended department store offenders was more than three times as large as that of postal thieves certainly supports Hall's position. However, the lower rate of trust violation in the Post Office may be attributable to factors quite unrelated to prosecution. As Civil Service employees, postal employees must pass certain standard examinations and they participate in various occupational, social, and personal advantages. Hall himself emphasizes that "the position provides security both in tenure and in retirement, and it carries the prestige of government employment" and that "accordingly, status, security, including pension, and perhaps a higher esprit de corps set off that vocation from many other comparable types of employment." [8]

REASONS FOR INFREQUENT PROSECUTION OF DISHONEST EMPLOYEES

The attitude of the public has long been one of opposition to the behavior of the "ordinary" thief. These offenders have values which conflict with the community's and thus create no serious divergence of opinion among community members concerning the desirability of strict enforcement of the law. In trust violation, however, we confront important differences which, Hall [9] believes:

[6] *Ibid.*, pp. 328–329.
[7] *Ibid.*, p. 331. This is a minimal figure because not all of the 263 "not prosecuted" cases had been disposed of.
[*] Rate of Post Office apprehensions calculated from figures in Hall, *loc cit.*, p. 328.
[8] *Ibid.*, p. 328.
[9] *Ibid.*, p. 304.

result from the wholesale violations among all strata of the community, aggravated by a consensus of opinion regarding the values involved, i.e., the embezzlers recognize that they are violating their own values. More important is the fact that when detected, they are treated sympathetically by those in control. Thus, in sum, embezzlement is wrong; everybody, including most embezzlers, recognize that, and there is no basic challenge to the rightness of the prevailing standards. But, far from rigorous law-enforcement by the "dominant class" when its property interests are criminally appropriated, we encounter condonation and wholesale avoidance of legal coercion. In sharp contrast to what we find regarding *known apprehended* thieves and criminal receivers (against whom there is ample evidence for conviction), in the case of the embezzlers, there is such lack of law-enforcement as to practically nullify the legal controls.

Similarly, Cavan has posited a continuum of conformity and nonconformity with respect to any type of criminal behavior, one of the elements of which consists of public tolerance of the behavior involved. Cavan believes that theft from retail stores by staff or shoplifters is characterized by a relatively high degree of public tolerance, thus reducing the probability of official action: "Only when a crime of the tolerated type is large, damaging to the business involved, or made known to the public is it likely to lead to arrest, trial, and legal punishment." [10] Many employers are genuinely sorry for the individual who has succumbed to temptation, feel that dismissal is sufficient punishment and, particularly if the offender's work history was good prior to the offense, prefer to avoid the disgrace to the employee and his family which would result from prosecution.[11] From a more practical viewpoint, the employer may be more concerned with simply eliminating the cause of profit loss than with revenge, especially if the defalcation is small and/or if further investment of time, money, and effort involved in prosecution is not economically justifiable. In this connection, Hall has theorized that the rate of prosecution of known offenders in general is positively related to the advantage which the complainant will receive by such action. In embezzlement,

[10] Ruth Shonle Cavan, "Underworld, Conventional and Ideological Crime," *Journal of Criminal Law, Criminology and Police Science* 55 (June, 1964), p. 235.
[11] Alex Lee Gregory, "Why Workers Steal," *Saturday Evening Post* 235 (November 10, 1962), p. 71.

for example, if prosecution will result in recovery which cannot be obtained otherwise, then, other things being equal, the tendency will be to prosecute. Or if nothing is to be lost by prosecuting nor to be gained by withholding prosecution, the rate will increase.[12] Perhaps one of the most important reasons for infrequent prosecution of thieving employees—and one related to the effect of public tolerance of various types of criminal behavior—is that the rate of prosecution will vary inversely with the extent of psychological and social identification of the public with the offender.[13] More so than in other forms of theft and in other types of offenses, such identification is possible in trust violation—another way of emphasizing that the trust violator does not come within the popular conception of "criminal." While it is true that embezzling bankers and public officials are taken as the models of success, accorded the greatest respect, and thus allow for the strongest identification and emulation, "the embezzler in shirt sleeves, the truck driver and warehouse employee, though they do not evoke such wide imitation, are respected members of their group. All are distinguished from the prototype of the 'criminal' to whom otherness and malevolence are attributed." [14] The very fact that the employer's and public's attitude toward trust violation and violators is ambivalent militates against prosecution. In addition, trust violation is often a reflection of a serious personal problem and the motive one with which it may be difficult not to sympathize. This factor is related to and augments the preceding one: "In sum, it is easy to understand, to identify oneself with and, thus, to condone the conduct of persons who resemble us and who were sorely beset by difficulties that trouble many decent persons." [15]

Although fear of a suit for false arrest or malicious prosecution brought by the employee against the employer is often given as a reason for not prosecuting, such fear of reprisal is a minor influence in the decision process and compared with much more potent considerations its influence would be negligible.[16] A much more direct influence is the employer's desire to avoid publicity regarding staff dishonesty, perhaps feeling that trust viola-

[12] Hall, *loc. cit.*, pp. 318–319.
[13] *Ibid.*, p. 318.
[14] *Ibid.*, p. 306.
[15] *Ibid.*, p. 307.
[16] *Ibid.*, p. 309.

tion reflects upon their ability to select honest and loyal workers. The image of a business, particularly a sizable one, is hardly improved by leaving itself open to the charge of persecuting, by prosecuting, defenseless employees who through circumstances beyond their control found it necessary to steal from the boss. Indeed, if trust violation were a simple expression of financial need, at least among department store workers the problem would be to explain, not why those who were caught had stolen, but, more importantly, why 99.5 per cent of the employee force did not violate their trust. Finally, it should be noted that only large concerns and corporations apprehend dishonest employees in sufficient number to make their disposition a problem. Even firms with a few hundred workers may go for years without detecting an employee pilferer. And it is precisely in the large corporation that the loss occasioned by trust violators is least personalized, as opposed to that in "ordinary" theft or in relatively small businesses where the internalized meaning of "ownership" has not completely disappeared. Whether recovery is obtained or not in large concerns, the enforcers of company policy and management continue to draw their weekly paychecks. Even when prosecution will not result in restitution for injury, a personal victim may prosecute in order to be "compensated" for his financial loss by the satisfaction of having the offender suffer just as the victim has —a kind of psychic restitution. However, the financial loss caused by dishonest employees normally is sustained by that nebulous entity *the company* rather than any *individual* within it.

DIFFERENTIALS IN DISPOSITION
OF COMPANY OFFENDERS

It has already been pointed out that in Companies A–C less than 1 employee in 5 was prosecuted, with Company B prosecuting 2 out of every 100, Company C 8 out of each 100, and Company A, 1 out of every 3. This section will explore the factors which influenced disposition of the trust violators, the bases upon which offenders were either discharged without further embarrassment to them or turned over to the police for prosecution. The analysis is restricted to Company A because it was the only firm among the three which prosecuted a sufficiently large number of employees to permit a statistical investigation of disposition. The disposition data of the three companies were not combined because each is a completely independent, autonomous organization and because of the large a priori differences in disposition between Company A and Companies B and C. Moreover, since 86 per cent of the offenders prosecuted by all three companies were Company A employees, the findings based upon Company A's prosecuted offenders could not have been appreciably altered had the 40 employees prosecuted by Companies B and C been included in the analysis.

Company A prosecuted a larger proportion of cleaners than offenders in any other position (see Table 1). Stock personnel

Table 1
Prosecution of Employees, by Position

Position	No. of Cases	Number Prosecuted	% Prosecuted
Sales	319	84	26.3
White Collar	70	26	37.1
Servicemen	142	51	35.9
Stock	88	35	39.8
Cleaners	46	28	60.9
Executive	74	24	32.4
Total	739	248	33.6

were the second most frequently prosecuted group, while sales embezzlers were least likely to be reported to the police. It is interesting to note in passing that in Companies B and C combined, cleaners also had the highest rate of prosecution (16 per 100 cleaners) and salespeople the lowest rate (less than 1 per 100 sales employees). Because the distribution of prosecuted offenders by position in A–C was radically different from that of all apprehended trust violators, and since many of the most significant variables connected with department store employee theft varied with position, any analysis of this phenomenon based upon an official sample of prosecuted cases would have been completely unrepresentative of the universe.

There was apparently no inclination on the part of Company A to be more lenient with female than with male violators: 17 per cent of those prosecuted were females, and females constituted 18 per cent of all apprehended employees. As hypothesized, a *significantly** smaller proportion of employees rated as excellent or good workers (27%) than those considered fair or poor (35%) were prosecuted. Also, a *significantly* smaller proportion of offenders who were with the company 5 years or more (28%) than those whose length of service was less than 5 years (34%) were prosecuted; the average length of service for prosecuted violators was 33 months compared with 41 months for those who were released. With respect to age, a larger proportion of dishonest employees 20 through 24 (41%) and a smaller proportion (21%) who were 45 years or older were prosecuted than were employees in any other age group; almost one third (31%) of the 18- and 19-year-old violators were reported to the police. The average age of prosecuted and released offenders was 29 years and 30 years, respectively. The following hypotheses concerning disposition were not supported: (1) that fewer married than single employees would be prosecuted. An identical proportion of both groups were prosecuted. The assumption that being married and having children contributes to a "solid-citizen" image, thus permitting greater identification with the thief by the enforcers of company policy was therefore not substantiated. (2) that a larger proportion of employees who denied their guilt would be prosecuted than those who admitted dishonesty. On the contrary, twice as many of the latter (35%) as of the former (18%) were prosecuted. (3) that a larger proportion of employees who ever stole with other employees would be prosecuted than solitary offenders. In fact, an identical proportion (34%) of collusive and solitary trust violators were prosecuted.

The "size-of-theft"—the total dollar value of merchandise and money ever embezzled by the employee during his employment —emerges as the single most important and decisive determinant of disposition. Nineteen per cent of those who stole less than $100 were prosecuted, compared with 57 per cent who stole $100 or more. Only 1 in every 10 dishonest employees who embezzled less than $20 was prosecuted, compared with one quarter of the trust

---

* When the word "significant" is italicized it refers to statistically significant differences at the .05 level of confidence or better. In the vast majority of tests where differences in proportions were significant at this level of confidence, they were also significant at the .01 or .001 level of confidence. For a discussion of the use of the chi-square test, see Marvin E. Wolfgang, *Patterns in Criminal Homicide* (Philadelphia: University of Pennsylvania Press, 1958), pp. 17–18.

violators whose size-of-theft was $20 to $100. The average amount stolen by prosecuted employees—$608—was three times as large as that of released offenders ($194). When amount stolen is held constant, among offenders who took $100 or more a *significantly* larger proportion of males (60%) than of females (47%) were prosecuted. This finding invalidates a reference above to the effect that Company A was apparently equally severe with female as with male violators. While such would seem to be the case initially, when the important factor of amount stolen was taken into consideration, the well-documented tendency for the enforcers of the legal order to be more lenient with women than with men is evidenced. Similarly, the tendency reported above for Company A to be more lenient with employees who were associated with the organization longer does not persist when size-of-theft is controlled: among those who stole $100 or more, the average length of service of prosecuted and released employees was 40 months and 41 months, respectively. However, even when the amount stolen is controlled, the hypothesis that more lower status employees (cleaners, servicemen, stock personnel) than higher status ones (executives, salespersons, white collar workers) would be prosecuted was confirmed: *a significantly* larger proportion of the former (73%) than of the latter (50%) were not released. Thus, *it has been possible to offer empirical evidence that the offenders with whom the enforcers can more easily identify are treated more sympathetically*—and what better way to express such identification and empathy with the trust violator than by not exposing him publicly.

Further documentation of the significance of the amount stolen in disposition comes from two sources: a comparison of the size-of-theft of prosecuted and released trust violators by position with that of all offenders by position, and an examination of the reasons given by Company A itself for not prosecuting, information which was recorded in two thirds of the cases. With respect to the first, the average amount stolen by prosecuted offenders in each position was considerably larger than the mean size-of-theft of released employees in the same position, ranging from twice as much among prosecuted cleaners to nine times as much among prosecuted stock personnel (see Table 2). Moreover, the ratio of the average amount stolen by prosecuted offenders in a particular position to that of the average size-of-theft for all of-

Table 2
Average Amount Stolen by Disposition, by Position

	Amount Stolen by	
Position	prosecuted cases	released cases
Sales	$ 387	$ 146
White Collar	$ 791	$ 298
Servicemen	$ 560	$ 263
Stock	$ 741	$ 82
Cleaners	$ 287	$ 144
Executive	$1522	$ 453
Total	$ 608	$ 194

fenders in other positions where the average amount stolen greatly exceeded that of all offenders in the former was considerably restricted. For example, the mean size-of-theft of *all* executive violators was four times larger than that of *all* salespeople but only twice as large as that of *prosecuted* salespeople. The average size-of-theft of *all* executives was 2.1 times that of *all* servicemen but only 1.5 times that of *prosecuted* servicemen. The average amount stolen by *all* clerks and cashiers was 1.5 times as much as that of *all* stock offenders but about one third *less* than that of *prosecuted* stock personnel, etc. Moreover, with only one clear exception, there was a tendency for *prosecuted* offenders in each position, on the average, to steal almost as much as or more than *released* offenders in other positions which had a much larger mean size-of-theft for *all* employees than the former did for all employees. To illustrate, *all* executive violators stole on the average 2.4 times as much as *all* stock pilferers, but *prosecuted* stock personnel stole 1.6 times *more* than *released* executives. Similarly, *all* cashiers and clerks embezzled 2.4 times the average size-of-theft of salespeople, but the mean amount stolen by *released* cashiers and clerks was only about three quarters that of *prosecuted* salespeople.

With respect to the second type of information on disposition, of the 338 cases in which the company's reasons for not prosecuting were known, 13 per cent were released because the amount stolen was considered trivial, in 6 per cent the District Attorney recommended against prosecution, 3 per cent were turned over to the military or juvenile authorities; 2 per cent were not prosecuted because of the technical legal problems involved, 7 per cent because of personal and/or family considerations, fewer than 1 per cent because their dishonesty was self-confessed, 9 per cent for "other" reasons, and 58 per cent because of insufficient evidence to secure a conviction. The average amount embezzled by the 45 offenders whose cases were considered trivial was $26—less than one twentieth of the mean size-of-theft of prosecuted employees. The average amount stolen by offenders not prosecuted because of insufficient evidence was $250, ten times that of trivial cases but still less than half of the average amount stolen by prosecuted offenders. Despite the company's explanation that it did not prosecute 197 dishonest employees because of insufficient evidence to assure a conviction— 87 per cent of whom admitted their trust violation in a signed statement—it is doubtful that all of these 197 offenders would have been prosecuted even if there had been sufficient evidence on which to do so. Rather, it is more logical to assume that the rate of prosecution in these cases would have been similar to that of all cases on the basis of the amount stolen. For example, 54 of the offenders who purportedly were released because of insufficient evidence stole less than $20. Company A, even if it had had incontrovertible proof of the guilt of these 54 employees, would hardly have prosecuted all of them. The reader will recall that the average amount stolen by offenders released because they took trivial sums and in which sufficient evidence to prosecute existed was $26; in addition, only 10 per cent of all trust violators who embezzled under $20 were prosecuted. Therefore, if it is assumed that the prosecution rate of offenders released because of insufficient evidence, in the absence of this deterrent, would have been the same as that of all offenders by amount stolen category, then approximately 62 of the 197 employees not prosecuted because of insufficient evidence *would have* been prosecuted, thereby increasing Company A's overall prosecution rate to 42 per cent and the proportion of offenders brought to official attention to 47 per cent. By extending this reasoning, where applicable, to employees who were not prosecuted for three other reasons, the logical inference is that Company A *would have* prosecuted 49 per cent and *would have* brought 53 per cent of its employees to official attention.

Finally, recovery characteristics were investigated in relation to disposition in order to determine what effect, if any, they had upon the decision to prosecute. Virtually all of the amount stolen by the 45 released offenders who pilfered trivial sums was recovered, compared with 85 per cent of the total value embezzled by prosecuted trust violators. Nevertheless, it cannot be inferred that *because* complete recovery was obtained from trivial cases they were not prosecuted; rather, it would be more plausible to maintain—and the position will be supported by empirical evidence to be presented shortly—that almost regardless of the amount recovered in relation to size-of-theft, the probability of Company A prosecuting employees who stole less than $100 was not more than 1 in 4. If the size-of-theft was below a certain value, Company A rarely considered it worthwhile to become involved in court proceedings. On the other hand, it would seem that the average amount stolen by employees released because of insufficient evidence ($250) was large enough to warrant prosecution in a substantial number of these cases, had other factors been equal. Moreover, only 52 per cent of the amount stolen by offenders released because of insufficient evidence was recovered, compared with 85 per cent of the amount stolen by prosecuted employees, suggesting that in the absence of insufficient evidence a certain number of them probably would have been prosecuted in order to obtain court-imposed restitution for their thefts or at least to punish them for their refusal to compensate the company for their defalcations. However, in 78 per cent of the 197 cases of employees released because of insufficient evidence, complete recovery of the amount stolen was obtained by the company. In other words, Company A maintained that although it incurred no known loss from 153 released offenders where complete recovery was obtained in every case, it would have prosecuted these 153 employees had there been sufficient evidence to obtain a conviction. This raises a most interesting and important question: to what extent did Company A prosecute employees where complete recovery had been obtained *prior* to legal action—in which case court-ordered restitution could not have been an objective of prosecution—and why? In 110 of the 136 cases of prosecuted offenders who were not ordered to make restitution by the court, complete recovery was obtained nonetheless. Since the court did not order any of these 110 dishonest employees to make restitution or specify it as a condition of their sentence, there would have been no reason for them to compensate the company *after* they were prosecuted, convicted, and sentenced and *as a result* of such legal action taken against them. Therefore, 110 offenders —45 per cent of those prosecuted—had made restitution or were cases in which complete recovery had been obtained prior to and/or independent of prosecution. Almost half of the trust violators, then, were prosecuted strictly for punitive rather than for economic reasons, *i.e.*, the company's purpose was to punish the employee for his violation of trust rather than simply to correct the financial injury by obtaining recovery, which had already been accomplished. Among convicted employees who were ordered to make restitution by the court, the proportion of the amount stolen which was recovered (92%) was larger than that recovered from violators who were not ordered to make restitution (79%). In addition, 96 per cent of the cases of convicted trust violators who were ordered to make restitution eventuated in complete recovery, compared with only 81 per cent of the cases of convicted offenders not ordered by the court to make restitution. On the basis of these facts—the proportion of the *amount* stolen which was recovered and the proportion of *cases* where complete recovery was obtained—there was greater recovery among convicted offenders who were ordered to make restitution by the court than in cases of convicted offenders where restitution was not imposed. This suggests that a large number of the 55 per cent of convicted employees were prosecuted for economic reasons, *i.e.*, to obtain restitution which was not forthcoming prior to prosecution. Of course, in view of the fact that 45 per cent of the employees in Company A were prosecuted for strictly punitive reasons, it is possible that had the remaining 55 per cent of prosecuted offenders also made complete restitution prior to being brought to court, they would have been prosecuted in any event, and that the prosecution of the 111 offenders who were ordered to make restitution by the court was prompted by both punitive and economic considerations. It may be concluded, therefore, (1) that the recovery characteristics were much less important determinants of disposition than the absolute size-of-theft, (2) that regardless of the proportion of the amount stolen which was recovered, if employees stole at least $100 and Company A believed that a conviction could be obtained, their chances of being prosecuted were better than even, and (3) that, assuming there was sufficient evidence to prosecute, their chances of being prosecuted increased directly with the amount pilfered and were virtually assured when a large amount was stolen and complete reparation was not obtained.

JUDICIAL DISPOSITION OF COMPANY OFFENDERS

Of the 259 prosecuted trust violators in Companies A–C who were tried, 256 or 99 per cent were convicted. This near-perfect conviction record was a result of very careful selection by department stores of whom and when to prosecute, further evidenced by the fact that Company A declined to prosecute 172 violators who had admitted their dishonesty in a signed statement because the company was not convinced that the evidence would sustain a conviction. In court 249 of the 259 offenders (96%) pleaded guilty.[17]

The judicial disposition of convicted offenders is an intrinsically interesting area and one that is highly significant because the court both molds and reflects public opinion. By examining

[17] Clinard also found a high rate of conviction among OPA criminal cases as a result of careful consideration before being turned over to the Department of Justice for prosecution, 93 per cent of the 12,415 completed criminal cases from 1942 to 1947 resulting in conviction. Clinard, *loc. cit.*, p. 239. See also Marshall B. Clinard, "Criminological Theories of Violations of Wartime Regulations," *American Sociological Review* 11 (June, 1946), p. 263. By contrast with these figures and those in the Department Store Study, the *Judicial Criminal Statistics* issued by the Census indicates that a higher proportion of offenders prosecuted for embezzlement and fraud were disposed of without conviction than in the prosecution of most serious offenses. In Illinois, as revealed by the Illinois Crime Survey statistics, a much larger proportion of embezzlement and fraud cases than any other crime was eliminated in the preliminary hearing, with over 70 per cent of such prosecutions in Chicago and Cook County eliminated at this level. Additional evidence on the low rate of convictions which is directly comparable to the concept of "trust violators" in the present study comes from the annual reports of the New York City Police Department, which includes statistics on violation of financial trust: from 1935 to 1947 inclusive, 4,059 to 7,938 "dishonest employees," or 51 per cent, were convicted. Only 42 per cent of the 1,754 offenders prosecuted for embezzlement and related defalcations in insured nonmember banks from 1935 through December, 1950 resulted in conviction; it should be noted that all such cases are turned over to U.S. district attorneys for disposition. It is clear that the greater selectivity and discretion exercised by private security personnel and company officials in department stores results in much more successful prosecution of the thieves which they apprehend than of offenders handled by our more conventional agencies of social control. See Hall, *loc. cit.*, pp. 320–322, 331.

the sentences administered by the courts to the 256 convicted violators of Companies A–C, some objective indices of society's attitude toward dishonest employees of the type represented in the DSS can be obtained and some interpretations offered.

Seventy-three, or 29 per cent, of the 256 convicted dishonest employees were fined. The average fine imposed was $72 for those who received any fine and $20 for all convicted offenders; one-quarter of the fines were for $100 or more. Forty-four per cent of the thieves were ordered to make restitution, the average amount being $637 in this group and $286 for all offenders. Among those ordered to make restitution, in 27 per cent of the cases the amount was under $100 and $500 or more in 29 per cent of the cases. Twenty-seven per cent of the 256 convicted trust violators were fined and ordered to make restitution only. Among those given any suspended sentence the average was 11 months, with two thirds given less than one year suspended sentence and only 9 per cent a suspended sentence of 3 years or more. In 55 per cent of the 256 cases the imposition of the sentence was suspended. Fifteen per cent of the offenders were given a definite suspended sentence and ordered to make restitution only. Forty-six per cent of the violators were placed on probation, for an average length of time of 17 months; of these, one third were placed on probation for more than one year. Almost one quarter were given a suspended sentence and placed on probation only; while one third were either given a suspended sentence or placed on probation only.[18] Thirty per cent of the 256 trust violators were placed on probation and ordered to make restitution only.

The most significant and striking finding was that only 12 of the 256 convicted department store trust violators—less than 5 per cent—were sentenced to and presumably served some time in prison; and in 9 of these 12 cases the length of imprisonment was 6 months or less. In other words, the court avoided imposing punitive sentences in 95 per cent of the cases. Moreover, the

---

[18] Between 1933–44, with the exception of persons convicted of auto theft and receiving stolen property, a larger proportion of offenders convicted of embezzlement or fraud were given a suspended sentence or placed on probation than in convictions of any other serious crime. In 43 per cent of the 741 cases of embezzlement or related defalcations in insured nonmember banks which resulted in conviction, probation or suspended sentence was imposed. Hall, *loc. cit.*, pp. 320, 331.

non-punitive sentences which were imposed could hardly be characterized as severe but instead were nominal and represented minimal judicial action against the trust violators: the fines were small, two-thirds being $50 or less, three-fifths of the definite suspended sentences were for 6 months or less, two thirds of those placed on probation were for one year or less and one quarter for 6 months or less. The most frequently imposed sentence, restitution, was in effect no more than a request by the court that the thief compensate the victim for his injury in direct proportion to the injury.

The leniency of the courts toward white collar criminals has been emphasized elsewhere on the basis that *only* 26 per cent of such offenders are imprisoned,[19] fully five times the proportion of dishonest department store employees who were deprived of their freedom. Why was the court so lenient with the department store offenders?—a condition which cannot be attributed to the idiosyncratic sentimentality of one or two judges since the convicted offenders were sentenced in 90 cities distributed throughout the United States. If the court is unwilling to impose severe sentences upon white collar criminals because of the nature of their offense and the relative absence of criminal records among the violators, this is equally if not more true of dishonest department store company offenders. It is of interest to note that only 2 per cent of Company A's trust violators had a prior record, considerably less than that among white collar criminals. If judges are reluctant to make criminals of reputable businessmen by sentencing them to prison,[20] they are certainly much more reluctant to make criminals of, if not reputable, at least respectable working men and women who steal from their employers. Hall is undoubtedly correct concerning the court's desire to avoid punitive measures if restitution is made.[21]

Although the lenient attitude of judges toward dishonest employees may be very similar, though not identical, with their attitude toward white collar criminals, the underlying reasons for such leniency are very different. One important reason for the

[19] Clinard, "Criminological Theories of Violations of Wartime Regulations," *loc. cit.* and *The Black Market, loc. cit.,* pp. 239–240. Even among bank embezzlers, approximately one quarter of those convicted are given punitive sentences. Hall, *loc. cit.,* p. 331.
[20] Clinard, *The Black Market, loc. cit.,* pp. 243–244.
[21] Hall, *loc. cit.,* p. 323.

virtual absence of punitive sentences imposed on the DSS offenders was perceptively raised by Hall in the form of a question in connection with embezzlement cases and is no less applicable to the department store offenders. He cites the court's belief that the function of corrective treatment made possible by imprisonment would be extremely limited if not meaningless, since the offenders are normal, reasonably competent, respectable working class people free of any association with criminals or criminal sub-cultures. To be sure, civil and criminal sanctions were occasionally imposed on the dishonest employees: restitution, nominal fines, and short-term probation. However, the very absence of the deterrent which middle class individuals fear most, imprisonment, and the substitution of largely financial measures, was tantamount to an admission by the court that it could do little *for* the offenders and that it chose to do nothing *to* them. Fines, restitution, and probation in a sense have their parallel in the white collar civil sanctions of damages, warnings, etc. Moreover, while the leniency of judges toward white collar criminals has been related to the former's membership in the same social strata as the latter, thus being considerably influenced by the opinion and power of the defendants,[22] the court certainly does not fear the power of department store employees, does not identify with them, and probably feels more sympathy than respect for them. The fact that five times as many white collar criminals as department store trust violators were sentenced to prison may reflect the court's great empathy with and indulgence of the transgressions of relatively powerless individuals who have so little and attempt to obtain a little more, albeit dishonestly, and the court's more critical attitude toward relatively powerful persons who already have so much and yet try for so much more illegally.

THE PRIVATE ADMINISTRATION OF JUSTICE

Perhaps more than any other civil individual, the employer or his corporate representatives are in a position where they must decide whether or not to report a known, apprehended offender to the law enforcement officials, a responsibility and power which has been largely ignored in the sociology of law. What effect does

[22] Clinard, *loc. cit.*, p. 245.

such discretion have upon the legal and moral order, upon the ethic of honesty which the law sustains, upon the offender himself and others like him? While any brief answer provided here must be less than definitive, at least some of the consequences of the private disposition of offenders can be explored. Essentially, the ability of the employer to prosecute or release as many or as few trust violators as he chooses and to decide who will and will not be formally charged with a crime must be analyzed within a trifold framework consisting of (1) the effect of such power upon the offender and public, (2) the objectives of punishment, *i.e.*, prosecution and sentencing, and (3) the victim.

In some respects the victim of a crime today is in a less favorable position than in an earlier time. "The number of victims may be assumed to have increased at the same rate as criminals, but there has been no improvement in the victim's lot to compare with the advances which have been made in criminology and certainly not to compare with the amelioration of the lot of the criminal which has taken place." [23] While the state attempts to protect society against crime, when a loss or injury is incurred there generally is no effective remedy to the individual victim, whose only satisfaction then derives from the punishment inflicted upon the criminal. As though in self-defense against this situation, the department store companies in the present study have attempted to find their own solution to employee dishonesty, one in which their own interests are given priority; that in a majority of cases they were able to obtain complete or considerable recovery without the aid of the court is an indication of their success in this regard. Even when restitution cannot be obtained by the employer without legal assistance, most probably prefer to avoid further investment of money and personnel in an employee's case which already has resulted in financial loss to the company and which, if prosecuted, might lead to a further net loss, thus in a sense perpetuating their own victimization. Clearly, from the standpoint of the employer, his first responsibility is to himself. Moreover, what would the function of prosecution be? If it were simply to obtain restitution which could not be obtained otherwise—to have the court do for them what they could not do for themselves—the criminal court would be cast into the role of

[23] Stephen Schafer, *Restitution to Victims of Crime* (London: Stevens & Sons Limited, 1960), p. 117.

a collection agency, no more and no less. This is not to suggest that restitution has no place in penology. On the contrary, making restitution is something which the offender does in order to atone for and correct his misconduct. As such, it may be viewed as the first step toward rehabilitation, as an admission by the offender that he has offended, that he is aware he has committed a crime and is willing to do something about it. Since restitution requires effort on the part of the offender, it may be particularly useful in strengthening his feelings of responsibility, while at the same time benefiting the victim.[24] There is reason to believe that *rectification* or *making good* is an equally effective disciplinary technique with grown-up criminals as it is with children, preventing repetition of misconduct and generating little resentment.[25] Accordingly, restitution may by utilized as a penal and reformative technique "through which guilt can be felt, understood and alleviated." [26] The question still remains, of course, whether privately obtained or court-imposed restitution is more beneficial to the offender. Restitution obtained by the employer without recourse to the law may allow the offender to interpret his behavior as a civil injury which can be easily corrected by reimbursing the victim, in much the same way that an overdue bill is attended to. On the other hand, restitution ordered by the court may add a necessary punitive element which confirms beyond a doubt the criminal character of the employee's behavior. However, whether restitution is obtained privately or by the court may be a subtle distinction having no differential effect upon the offender who, under either circumstance, welcomes restitution as an opportunity to "buy his way out" of criminal responsibility. Moreover, it is doubtful whether the court itself in imposing restitution does so as part of a sound peno-correctional program rather than merely adopting the lay point of view of most employers. If this is the case, *i.e.,* if the role of restitution does not appreciably vary with how it is obtained, and given the absence of punitive sentences administered to the DSS offenders, it may well be asked what the function of prosecution is with trust violators. By Hall's own admission, it is arguable that the power of employers to prosecute often or infre-

[24] *Ibid.,* p. 125.
[25] *Ibid.,* p. 126.
[26] *Ibid.*

quently and to select who shall be immune from contact with
the law is "after all, the best one among practicable alternatives,"
and further that the practices and attitudes which such a situation engenders "as well as their consequences, are socially desirable, that, in effect, we have an enlightened private individ-
ualization of treatment which avoids the crudities of exposure
and punishment and, in sum, is superior to official administration
of the criminal law." [27] Not prosecuting trust violators is humane
in that the individual does not become a man with a "record." In
effect, the offender is punished for his crime by being discharged
—no small loss for middle class persons, who then find it more
difficult to obtain new employment—and at the same time is
given another chance at respectability. Unfortunately, it is unknown whether prosecuted trust violators make better adjust-
ments to their future employment situations and are in general
more law-abiding as a result of such public exposure and conviction than those not prosecuted. In a majority of cases, being apprehended and interrogated by detectives or company officials,
followed by accusation, admission of dishonesty, and dismissal
may be a highly effective deterrent to further criminal behavior
while still providing the offender an opportunity to salvage his
future and learn from his past mistake. If minimal sanctions can
accomplish the same objective as more severe ones, one may
again ask what is to be gained by prosecution. This is not to
overlook the possibility that some released offenders may be in
the early stages of a criminal career, that other employers may
expose themselves unknowingly to similar victimization, perhaps
by placing the individual in a position surrounded by tempta-
tions to which he is most vulnerable, or that if the behavior arose
from deep, unresolved personal problems such problems are simply avoided rather than confronted by releasing the offender—
conditions which presumably would be subject to more successful treatment if the individual were prosecuted. In addition, conviction in itself would make it more difficult for trust violators
to rationalize their behavior in order to continue thinking of
themselves as respectable citizens. As officially convicted criminals, the immorality and illegality of their conduct would be
forcefully impressed upon them as perhaps would otherwise not
be the case. In support of the case for prosecution, Hall has

[27] Hall, *loc. cit.,* p. 341.

pointed out that rehabilitation is not the *only* objective of the criminal law and penology and that, assuming that conviction and correction (imprisonment) were not rehabilitative or no more so than private disposition of the offender, the fact of being arrested and charged with a crime has important implications for the deterrence of other trust violators and, more crucial, for the reinforcement of the transgressed values.[28]

. . . an important, though certainly not exclusive, place in any adequate treatment program for embezzlers must be reserved for the moral instruction provided by just punishment. What is basic in this viewpoint is the importance of careful public evaluation of the offender's conduct—with congruent consequences. This implies that the punishment is deserved in the sense that the offender is a normal adult who could and should have controlled his criminal drives.

Nevertheless, there are always discrepancies between the legal order, public attitudes, and law-enforcement practices. The inclination to take legal action against offenders not for rehabilitation purposes nor to protect society but to reaffirm values and have the offenders serve as examples is becoming less acceptable. Neither society, the writer, nor, based upon the judges' disposition of the convicted DSS offenders, the court would agree that every individual who commits a crime should be subject to official attention. The nature of the offense and characteristics of the offender are legitimate factors to consider in disposing of the offender. Reporting to the police and the prosecution of *all* individuals who commit *any* crime may be less justifiable than the automatic release of all trust violators. How many would agree, for example, that employees who take their employer's stamps and stationery for personal use, which of course legally constitutes theft, should be reported to the authorities? If any sanction is imposed, reproach is generally considered adequate in relationship to the "offense" and "offender." The theft of merchandise proper and cash, considered much more serious, invariably meets with a more severe sanction: dismissal. To be sure, the private administration of justice even on a small scale does contain elements of injustice and is not being prescribed as a substitute for

[28] *Ibid.*, p. 334.

traditional legal structures. Perhaps more than anything else this discussion and dilemma highlights the fact that in disposing of offenders, consideration of the victim, the objectives of punishment, and the power of the employer over trust violators are not all perfectly integrated but rather are characterized by conflict and ambivalence; yet, such strain among the parts is perhaps an inevitable, if not wholly desirable, reflection of our social system.